PALE GREEN
LIGHT ORANGE

PALE GREEN
LIGHT ORANGE

A Portrait of Bourgeois Ireland, 1930–1950

NIALL RUDD

THE LILLIPUT PRESS

First published in 1994 by
THE LILLIPUT PRESS LTD
4 Rosemount Terrace, Arbour Hill,
Dublin 7, Ireland.

Acknowledgments
The Lilliput Press receives financial assistance from
An Chomairle Ealaíon / The Arts Council, Ireland

A CIP record for this
title is available from
The British Library.

ISBN 1 874675 21 X

Set in 10 on 13 Janson Text by
❧ mermaid turbulence ❧
Printed in Dublin by
Colour Books of Baldoyle

Contents

Illustrations are on pp. 24, 44, 88 & 160

hoc est
uiuere bis, uita posse priore frui

Thinking of the past with pleasure
Brings of life a double measure

MARTIAL

Dublin

The sound of heavy engines filled the air until the house seemed to tremble. 'Ma'am! Ma'am! Will ye come and look at the airship!' It was Maggie's voice coming up from outside the back door. My mother hurried down, and I dashed after her, just in time to see the huge cigar shape moving slowly across the houses of Clontarf and out into Dublin Bay. Records show that this was the ill-fated R101 on a trial run over Ireland on the morning of Monday 18 November 1929.[1] I was then two years old and five months. The house was 'Lissadell', No. 13, Haddon Road, half-way up on the left. Far from having 'great windows, open to the south', like the Gore-Booths' residence in Sligo, our Lissadell was a red-brick semi with a bay window and a small front garden fenced in with black iron railings. The only exotic feature was a tall, sad and rather grimy palm-tree that faced you as you came through the side-passage. Behind that was a greenhouse with the remains of a grape-vine, and then a medium-sized garden with a lilac, an apple-tree and, at the end, a rowan, which I used to climb. Beyond the lane at the back was old Mr Kennedy's field; and sometimes the owner himself was to be seen, with hat, overcoat and a long staff, walking slowly around the field behind his cows.

'Maggie' was Maggie Gannon from Tullamore, some sixty miles west of Dublin. She was probably in her early thirties, but as far as I was concerned she belonged simply to the category of 'grown-up'. She had a bedroom in the back of the house, reached by a separate staircase with high uncarpeted wooden steps. On one of my rare visits I noticed a gaily coloured jug and basin. On the wall was a picture of the crucified Christ, with a large sacred heart in the bottom left-hand corner. On the dressing-table stood a bottle of holy water that I got into trouble for spilling. Once a week, on her evening off, Maggie's friend, Greta, would call to collect her; and then they would walk briskly down the road, looking very smart in their hats and gloves and high-heeled shoes. On other evenings I would often sit on the kitchen table while Maggie blacked the range or cleaned the silver. As she worked, she sang

> There's a little brown road winding over the hill,
> To a little white cot by the sea,
> And a little green gate at whose trellis I'll wait,
> While two eyes of blue come smilin' through at me...
>
> And if ever I'm left in this world all alone,
> I shall wait for my call patientlee;
> And if heaven be ki-ind, I shall wake there to fi-ind
> Those two eyes of blue still smilin' through aat mee.

This seemed to fit well enough with what I could gather from the teachings of Irish Methodism; and yet I knew that in some respects Maggie was different. She had that red heart and the holy water, and we didn't. Moreover, she went to mass and confession. What *was* mass? And what did you have to confess? From time to time I wondered about such questions, but something told me it would be rude to ask her. Meanwhile Maggie continued to sing, and when I was about seven I began to accompany her on a melodeon which I had been given for Christmas. It was a poor return for all this artistic co-operation when one day I locked her in the pantry and tip-toed away to shrieks of 'Ma'am!'. Later, much worse, I accidentally discharged a ·22 rifle in the playroom above the kitchen. Luckily the bullet simply went through the carpet and embedded itself in a joist, and no one knew anything about it. If nothing worse, it might easily have brought down a chunk of plaster on Maggie's head, and then she would have complained vehemently to 'the Master'.

'The Master' was not my father, but my maternal grandfather, Mr James H. Cooke. This old gentleman, now well on in his nineties, rented Lissadell from Mr Gore-Grimes, who used to come at regular intervals, dressed in a bowler hat and decent black, to discuss the maintenance of the property. Grandpa was born in 1841 in Gorey, Co. Wexford, into a family which had lived on the same farm continuously since 1630. Like the Websters, the Foleys, the Fiddlers, and some others, the Cookes had been brought over from Newbury in Berkshire when Bishop Ram acquired land in the area of Gorey and wanted some English yeomen to work it. The original farmhouse at Ballytegan seems to have lasted to the end of the eighteenth century. All that remains of it now is a pile of stones. The present building dates from that time, but was extended and renovated in the 1940s. One piece of family history concerns the rising of 1798, in which Co. Wexford was bitterly involved. A certain Father Stafford, who was being pursued by the authorities, took refuge in Ballytegan. The Cookes hid him and then provided a white horse for his escape. Before long, the situation was reversed. As the rebels closed in, the Cookes had to vacate their home and flee to Arklow. When eventually they returned, nothing had been touched, not even a jug of cream in the dairy. Hence the family tradition that there should always be a white horse at Ballytegan.

While still a boy, James Cooke was apprenticed to a draper's shop in West Street, Drogheda. To get there he had to walk behind a cart to Greystones, where the railway began, about twenty miles south of Dublin. Over the next ten or twelve years he must have applied himself to other things as well as his trade; for he succeeded in marrying Miss Alice Davis, the boss's daughter, and thus entering the Victorian commercial middle class. Not all can have gone smoothly. In my time there were stories of how the Hibernian Lace Company had been formed in partnership with the rascally Mr Andrews, who later absconded with the company's funds. But Grandpa must have recovered reasonably well. When I remember him he had long been a director of Arnotts; he had shares in the railways when they were worth having; and he had sufficient money to give his eldest daughter a house, round the corner in Victoria Road, as a wedding present.

James Cooke in his nineties was a small round jovial man with a fringe of white hair, clear blue eyes, and a set of flashing dentures. Considering that he had to have a weekly injection of insulin, he remained remarkably fit. Every Saturday he would watch rugby in Clontarf; on Sundays he attended the Methodist church at the bottom of St Lawrence Road; and on other days, when he didn't go into town, he would wander down to a garden seat on the sea front, which had been installed there for him by the flamboyant and energetic mayor, Alfie Byrne (for cartoons, see *Dublin Opinion* for the 1930s and 1940s *passim*). There he would engage passers-by, telling them stories about Wexford life in the years of the fam-ine, and about 'Drogheda', which he always pronounced with three syllables to sound almost like Drockeda. Like many people with an oral rather than a literary education, he had an excellent memory, and he would tell his stories with an almost formulaic accuracy. Some had the timelessness of folk-tales, like the one which concluded, 'He remembered the fine gold ring he'd seen on her finger as she lay in the coffin. So he said to himself "Wouldn't it be a shame, now, for a grand bit of gold like that to lie with her in the tomb to the last trumpet, when I could be getting a few good pounds for it from Orgel the jeweller?" So he waited till dusk, and then took a lamp and went down into the vault. He had opened the coffin and was coaxing the ring off, when all of a sudden didn't the woman herself sit up? He dropped the lamp and ran out into the street, howlin' like a dog. And he was never seen again.'

Grandpa always wore a grey suit with a short tailcoat; a gold watch-chain hung in a loop across his tummy. In bad weather he would strap on a pair of shiny black leggings – at least when I first knew him. Later he abandoned the leggings, but he never wore shoes – always a pair of black boots, which I would remove, easing them off his swollen feet when he slumped into his armchair before the fire. Not that I was always the dutiful grandson. Once someone gave me a joke knife with a blade which retracted into the handle. Without considering the effect on a nonagenarian, I crawled silently up beside his chair, rose on my knees, and brought it down with a yell on the rounded belly. Then, with a mixture of guilt and excitement, I leaned back to watch as the old man nearly shot out of the chair.

'Jamesie', as he was disrespectfully called by his daughters (behind his back), was a gentle, long-suffering character; and (presumably ever since those early days in Drogheda) he had been dominated by his strong-minded wife. Alice, as she was called, died in 1936 at the age of eighty-six. Slim and straight, with her white hair gathered in a bun, she completely ignored the changing fashions, climbing onto tramcars wearing a bonnet and a long brown satin dress with a full skirt, much embroidered. My father, who lived in the house perforce, because my mother accepted the duty of nursing her parents, never much liked his mother-in-law. He once told me *sotto voce*, 'The old lady can be damned cantankerous. This morning she turned poor old Jamesie out of the W.C.' Still, my grandparents stayed together, as of course one did in those days, and in 1938 James H. duly joined his wife in St Fintan's graveyard on the side of Howth hill, looking south across Dublin Bay. A baptismal font was placed in the church in their memory with the simple inscription, 'They served their day and generation'.

By the mid-1930s cars were becoming quite numerous. But there was still a fair amount of horse traffic. Every spring at the show grounds in Ballsbridge there was a splendid event in which a score or more of Dublin firms entered a competition; prizes were given to the best-turned-out teams. Merville Dairy, Tedcastle's Coal, Boland's Bakery, Johnston, Mooney and O'Brien, the Swastika Laundry, and many more, would come trotting past the stand, the horses with shining coats and brasses, the vehicles freshly painted, and the drivers in their smartest uniforms. Cattle were sometimes to be seen in the streets, especially near the market in the North Circular Road. Occasionally the odd beast would be driven up Haddon Road. Once my mother heard a shout from downstairs, 'Ma'am! Ma'am! Come quick. There's a cow in the kitchen!' 'Maggie, are you out of your mind?' But Maggie was right, except that, as mother came down, the cow had left the kitchen and was entering the drawing-room. Eventually it was driven out the door, but not before it had smashed the hall stand and emptied its capacious bowels on the drawing-room carpet. Mother went out to interview the drover, and she was still there, speechless with indignation, when my aunt and I came up the road. 'Well what did he have to say for himself?' asked my aunt, when the outlines of the tale had eventually been told. 'All he said was "Weren't you the right eejit to leave the door open?"'

At the age of five I was sent to a little school run by Miss Maud McKittrick, MA, and her sister Miss Florence in their bungalow at the end of Belgrove Road less than a mile away. A new road (Kincora Road) had just been built, with beautifully smooth pavements; so one could make fast time on a scooter or a pair of skates. Classes began at 9; there was a break before 11, and the academic rigours ended at lunch-time. The school was quite new; my cousin, Joan Polden, had been amongst the first batch admitted in the previous year. So we got plenty of individual attention. The singing was all right – we learned several songs and carols. But, for me, the handwork classes were a tiresome failure. I wrapped coloured raffia around a cardboard napkin-ring, and the result looked like an experiment designed to test the manual dexterity of a young chimpanzee. In three years I also made about a quarter of a rug, pulling bits of red and brown wool with a special needle through the holes in a square of canvas. Eventually Joan completed it, and the exact row at which bungler gave way to artist was painfully evident. The best part of the syllabus was the reading, but we also learned poetry by heart: "'Crom Cruach and his subgods twelve"/Said Cormac "are but carven treene./The axe that made them, haft or helve,/Had worthier of our worship been.'" In other words Samuel Ferguson's 'The Burial of King Cormac'. We also learned about Finn MacCumaill and his great band of warriors, the Fiana – which suggests that, unlike our West-Briton families, Miss McKittrick wanted us to know something about Ireland. At home I was given King Arthur and Robin Hood, followed by *The Jungle Book*. (After nearly sixty years, memories of the White Seal and Rikki Tikki Tavi still awaken excitement.) There were also some books in a big mahogany case in my playroom; but they seemed to belong to a much drearier world. At the age of about ten I got around to *Pilgrim's Progress*, and enjoyed it well enough. But I threw down *Eric, or Little by Little*, and I could never face the heroic story of *Mary Slessor of Calabar*. So I did not acquire much in the way of Victorian piety; and I have done nothing to make up for it since.

Miss McKittrick's was a cosy, civilized, place – perhaps slightly over-protective. But a few guilty memories suggest that the two ladies would not have been sorry to see me leave. First, there was the time when old Mrs McKittrick found me picking shiny pebbles out of her pebble-dashed wall, and reacted as though I was pulling down the house. More serious was the fact that my friend and contemporary, Peter Comley (an English boy with blond curls) used to suffer periodic nose-bleeds. Since these tended to occur in struggles with me, they were attributed, not always justly, to my savagery. There was also an episode, which calls for no comment in a post-Freudian age, when I pushed a dandelion up classmate Lorna's nose. At the end of term, that led to a very cool entry in my report: 'Conduct, fair', which caused an almighty row at home. In the school itself, every delinquency was punished by a black mark. More than three black marks in any one week meant that the culprit missed 'story', last period on Friday. The book being read that term was Anna Sewell's *Black Beauty*, which I liked. But after frequent banishments the narrative became so incoherent that I had to get hold of a copy and read it myself.

The small community in Miss McKittrick's all came from the Protestant Dublin middle class. There were denominational differences, but we were scarcely aware of them and didn't know what they meant. Outside school, however, the situation was different. If you turned right at the top of Haddon Road you were still in a late Victorian area; if you turned left, you were in a row of corporation houses. While there was seldom any overt hostility, the two groups of children did not play together. One of the other lot, a seven-year old like myself, once asked what my father earned. When I said I had no idea, he took a drag on his Woodbine, holding it with the lighted end pointing inward towards his palm, and said, 'Mine gets £360'. But whatever their income, the parents must have brought up their children pretty well; for there was no vandalism, and the stealing never went further than a few apples from the garden.

Clontarf Road ran along the edge of an inner recess of Dublin Bay. When the tide was in, the sea came up to the wall; and on stormy days the waves would hurl sheets of spray across the tram-lines. In the mid-30s it was decided to reclaim a strip of land; so a firm of Dutch engineers built a concrete wall just beyond the old stone one, and then another similar wall a hundred yards further out. The intervening space was then filled with sludge pumped in by dredgers. All this took several years, but in the end a layer of topsoil was added, grass was sown, and a pleasant promenade appeared. When the process started, you could climb over the stone wall, down into the valley between it and the first of the two concrete structures. Along the bottom was the slimy edge of the old sea bed, covered with weedy boulders, and water still seeped in with the tide. If you dug your nails into the filthy grey mud and hauled at a stone, it would come away with a damp sucking sound, often revealing a big dirty-green crab crouching underneath. While crab-hunting, I came to know Tom Sweeney. Three years or so older than me, he had dark wavy hair and wore a light blue jersey. Even then he had a certain self-contained strength. I had sometimes seen 'the kids' taunting him, and wondered why he didn't answer back or run away. 'Oh I just ignore them,' he said, 'and after a while they get fed up.'

As our friendship grew, Tom, who lived in a basement flat on the sea front, would come to play cricket in the garden of Lissadell. Most days it was an English county match, with personnel drawn from the cricket reports in the daily paper. I often opted for Gloucester, because of Wally Hammond, or Notts, so that I could be Joe Hardstaff. But I had great difficulty in coping with Tom's Yorkshire, especially when Bill Bowes joined the attack. On special occasions we held a full-dress test match, usually for the ashes; but sometimes South Africa (with stalwarts like Nourse and Wade) took the place of Australia. Fours were easily had in the smallish garden, but sixes were heavily discouraged. 'If you sky it into Headons' you lose a wicket; if it goes into Mulroy's you're all out.' As well as being an excellent playmate, Tom conveyed hints of a larger world. One day he said 'Last night some of us from school went to see the military tattoo. It was great gas.' 'You mean you were in town in the *dark*?' 'Yep. And on our way home we dropped into a café and had fish and chips for supper.' Fish and chips in town at night! By heaven, that was really living! On another occasion he confided, without arrogance, that his motto was 'speed and efficiency'. I had never heard of anyone having a motto before; it was clear that Sweeney was going places. (He did indeed; after qualifying as a doctor he spent many years in Kenya and then returned to an important medical post in England.)

The house to which ours was joined was occupied by the black-satin-busted Mrs Mulroy, a wild-haired, wild-eyed woman, liberally rouged. No one ever mentioned Mr Mulroy. Perhaps he had taken the wings of the morning. Or was he perhaps immured somewhere deep in the recesses of the house? At any rate, Mrs M. and her two bizarre lodgers made a menacing trio, with whom my relations were never easy. One day I watched from the front window as a cab drew up. The driver got out and assisted his passenger, a narrow red-faced man with thick glasses, a check cap, and a loosely flapping raincoat, to the gate. He then drove away, leaving the man (whom I knew to be called John O'Donaghue) draped over the gate in a strangely limp posture. In due course O'Donaghue began to move slowly and unsteadily towards the door. But once he had abandoned the support of the gate his knees buckled and he slumped to the ground, flattening a small shrub in the grass border. I watched aghast as he groped around for his glasses and started to crawl up the front steps. At that moment the hall door opened and Mrs Mulroy grabbed him by his coat collar. 'In witcha now. I'd say you'd had more than *wun* over the eight!'

That, and a few similar incidents, counted against them. But I, too, had a couple of things to answer for. One day I came across a powerful, stainless-steel catapult belonging to my father. Its black rubber sling was a quarter of an inch thick, and there was a nice leather pouch to hold the missile in place. After some practice with windfall apples, I found the weapon surprisingly accurate. I then turned and looked up at the window of Mrs Mulroy's back bedroom, whose sash was always about two feet open. With delight and amazement I watched as one rotting apple after another flew through the open space and vanished in the darkness beyond. But then my luck ran out. Choosing a larger and heavier apple, I let fly as before, but failed to allow for the extra weight. And so, with a kind of high-pitched tinkle, it went right through the glass.

That was bad. But worse was the time I saw, standing at the kerb, the Y-model Ford which belonged to the other lodger, Mr Herbie Brennan. As an official of some description, Mr Brennan wore a very dark grey suit, and covered his bald head with a kind of sub-Homburg hat. His faintly smirking mouth was surmounted by a pencil-thin moustache; and one felt that the entire effect could have been removed with the aid of a damp face-cloth. Why these hostile emotions should have surfaced when I had a piece of chalk in my pocket, I cannot tell. But without thinking, I tried to write an inscription on the door of his car. I could feel that the chalk was not adhering properly to the glossy paintwork, so to aid legibility I duplicated the inscription on the pavement beside the running-board. Admittedly part of my purpose was to try out an excremental monosyllable that had recently entered my vocabulary. But it was imprudent to connect the word with one who was certainly Mr Brennan's landlady, and (for all I knew) his mistress besides. Action followed quickly. Luckily my mother was out; but Maggie innocently called me to the door, where I was seized by Herbie Brennan and bundled into the next house. Twenty minutes later, after a terrific roasting, I was thrown out, convinced that I had narrowly escaped being sent to prison.

The Headons on the other side were totally different. Mr Headon was a former member of the Royal Irish Constabulary. He and his wife had six children, including a priest, a nun, and two doctors. Paddy, the younger of the doctors, was about fifteen years older than me. I can picture him standing in his garden and smiling up at my mother who was at an upstairs window. 'Great news!' he called. 'Mamma has just won a bet. She had a shilling on Golden Miller!' (Golden Miller won the Grand National in 1934.) Paddy must have joined the army immediately after qualifying, for he was taken prisoner at Tobruk. Tommy, the youngest, was still ten years older than me, but he was full of fun, and quite willing to play with me in the garden. Unusually large and powerful for his age, Tommy became the Dublin Schools' champion in the field events. In summer, as athletics meetings drew near, the ground would shake under the impact of the shot. His winter sport was rugger, and some years later, in 1939, he played in the front row for Ireland. With all his gaiety and insouciance, Tommy had a keen intelligence. After taking a science degree at University College Dublin, he went into industry, and was managing director of Urney's Chocolates when he died prematurely in his forties.

To a social historian it would have been obvious that while my family had entered the professional middle class in the generation before mine (my Uncle Ernest was a doctor), they had then remained more or less stationary, whereas the Sweeneys and the Headons had entered the same class in my generation. Hence my

Catholic playmates and I were on the same footing. Yet I could dimly sense that things were more complicated than that. Maggie, and other people in her position, always seemed to be Catholics. On the other hand, Dr and Mrs Burke who lived across the road were also Catholics. I once heard mother say that their daughter Mary, who had been to see *As You Like It*, was 'a very cultivated girl'. None of my connections cared about Shakespeare. So here were Catholics with superior tastes to ours. Well well. Again, one afternoon mother and I were invited out to Stillorgan to see the Hacketts – Catholic friends who had previously lived in Clontarf. But Mrs Hackett was a Scot; Mr Hackett was a schools inspector from Ulster, who wrote a book entitled *Bernard versus Shaw*; and in the company that afternoon were members of the de Valera family. Finally, the Sloans, Church of Ireland Protestants, who also lived on Haddon Road, were better off than we were. Their son, Stanley, who was about my age, had a magnificent car, which stood to mine as limousine to jalopy; his loft also housed a shiny and complicated system of electric trains, which ran on three-foot-high trestles in an area almost the size of the floor. One day, when he was in our garden, it occurred to me that it would be fun to pour a stream of water onto the gutter of the wash-house roof, and to watch it come rushing out at the bottom of the down-pipe before vanishing into the shore. 'Stanley, if you stand just there and keep your eye on the bottom of the pipe, I'll tip this bucket of water into the gutter.' But the load turned out to be heavier than I thought, and as I tottered down the sloping corrugated-iron roof I found myself gathering momentum; by the time I reached the gutter I could no longer control the bucket, and Stanley, who was gazing at the ground as requested, got the full cascade on the back of his neck.

The Clontarf Methodist Church was (and is) a fine grey-stone building on the corner of Clontarf and St Lawrence Road. My earliest memories are of walking through the door in my Sunday suit, past Uncle Stan (Mr Stanhope Polden), who as Circuit Steward stood at the entrance greeting members of the congregation, handing out hymn-books, and directing visitors to their places. Like grandpa, he had a gold watch-chain across his waistcoat. In the pew one was surrounded by red cushions and varnished wood, and up on the pale green wall was a white marble tablet with black writing. My parents and I were in the second last pew on the right. Behind us were my cousins, the Poldens, no doubt so that Uncle Stan could dodge in and out on his stewardly duties. Now the trouble was that, as Sunday school was in the afternoon, there was no arrangement for children to leave halfway through the service. The result was agonies of boredom. The hymns were all right for about three verses ('Methodism was born in song'). But the words were meaningless to a six-year-old, and some phrases caused trouble for many years. 'There is a green hill far away, without a city wall'. But why should a green hill *have* a city wall? In the noble revivalist hymn 'Yield not to temptation' we sang, 'Fight manfully onwards; dark passions subdue.' 'Passions', naturally, meant nothing. Nor had I heard 'subdue' in ordinary speech. I did, however, associate it aurally with those jelly fruits, lightly dusted with sugar, which were known as 'jube-jubes'. So I vaguely assumed that gluttony was under attack. This guess, perhaps, was in the right general area; but of course in the tradition of Victorian Puritanism 'passion' meant, almost exclusively, sex, and sex could not be mentioned at all. (Years later, I learned that even 'passion' had become so highly charged that, in the lines of the wedding hymn, 'love with every passion blending, pleasure than can never cloy', the word 'passion' had been replaced by 'feeling' – which, when you come to think of it, pretty well destroys the sense, as love is already a feeling.) Between the hymns came long improvised prayers, during which the congregation would bend forward in their seats. The first time I was taken to a Church of Ireland service I noticed that people actually *knelt* to pray. No one explained this, and I was left to conclude that it was in some way connected with other superstitious features, like white vestments, stained-glass windows, and the Book of Common Prayer.

Half-way through, the minister would announce 'the stewards will wait upon you for your offering' – a formula of such courtesy that it sounded like a relic of the eighteenth century. Uncle Stan then came down the aisle with a silver plate. By the time it reached us, it contained lots of shillings and a few half crowns. I added my mite, after checking whether it was 'heads or tails' or 'hens and harps'. A sweet was smuggled into my hand to stop me fidgeting during Mr Morton's sermon. This was always the worst part – forty minutes of florid declamation coming from a tall white-haired man in the pulpit. Even Uncle Stan's attention would wander, and, being a cashier in the Ballast Office, he would mentally tot up the numbers on the hymn-board. Then, becoming more restive, he would take out his gold hunter and spring it open and snap it shut, holding it up so as to catch the preacher's eye. But it never did any good. I sometimes think that the seeds of unbelief were planted in those early days when my most fervent prayers ('Oh God, please make Mr Morton stop!') went unanswered.

The most joyful service was the harvest festival, when the church was lavishly decorated withall kinds of flowers, fruit and vegetables. I sometimes wondered where all the produce came from, since there weren't any farms in Clontarf; but I happily became a countryman for the day and sang 'We plough the fields and scatter/The good seed on the land'. What happened to all the stuff afterwards? Somebody said it went to the city hospitals. So one imagined patients smiling gratefully as huge vegetable marrows, stooks of corn, and baskets of potatoes were dumped on their beds. The most sombre occasion was Remembrance Sunday, when we all wore poppies, and ex-servicemen, like Mr Comley, Mr Chambers, and Mr Mercier, wore their medals. My father also wore two medals, but on the other side of his jacket, since they belonged to my uncle Billy, who had been killed at Beaumont Hamel during the battle of the Somme in 1916. He had joined up soon after leaving Wesley College; so he was still barely twenty. In those services we sang 'For all the saints, who from their labours rest', to which there are a couple of fine tunes. Well, I don't suppose any of those lads were exactly saints; but in that battle alone over 400,000 British troops died, in circumstances of unimaginable horror. Looking back even now, when another calamity lies bet-ween, one can only stand in awe of what they did and suffered. So in those remembrance services, only fifteen years or so after the guns had fallen silent, one could still sense the heaviness of people's thoughts. Years later, when I read *All Quiet on the Western Front*, I realized that the Germans had experienced the same horror. But that only made the whole thing seem more appalling.

After the service, visiting preachers would often be entertained to lunch at Lissadell. A very early memory has to do with a hearty young clergyman called Mr Boyd. After eyeing him with some concern as he tucked into the roast beef, I leant forward from my high chair and repeated a maxim heard many times: 'Chew it well, Mr Boyd!' Usually, after lunch, as any kind of sport was forbidden ('Remember the Sabbath day to keep it holy'), there was nothing left to do except to make a nuisance of oneself. My father had the rather primitive idea that the naughtiness resided in my blue suit; for I was always at my most unbearable when wearing it. Another thing that wrecked his Sunday afternoon peace was the sound of 'Love's old sweet song' ('Just a song at twilight, when the lights are low...') played rather unsteadily on the cornet by a street musician. This always led to an outburst of bad language, as he threw down the Sunday paper and turned up the volume of the wireless. There was another musician, however, a singer appropriately named Carroll, who used to come round on Tuesday evenings. My mother said he had the remains of a good voice, and when he was heard I would take a penny from her purse in the sideboard, and run out into the dusk and give it to him. He always broke off in mid phrase and said 'Ah, God bless ye'. Once, when mother was out, I heard Carroll's voice coming up the road. So I ran to the sideboard. But when I opened the purse there were no pennies, only a silver-coloured coin of about the same size with a horse on it. This was unusual, but clearly Carroll could not be ignored. So I rushed out and handed him the coin. 'Ah, God bless ye,' he said. And then 'Hey now, what's this? Would she be wanting change?' 'No, no thanks!' I said airily, and dived back indoors.

The Sunday afternoon problem was solved when I was old enough for Sunday school. This fell into three parts: all pupils met together for hymn and prayer; then dispersed into groups for Bible-study; and then returned for a closing hymn. The first hymn was often 'All things bright and beautiful...' But I do not remember the bit that said 'The rich man in his castle, the poor man at the gate, he made them high and lowly; he ordered their estate'. Some democratically minded committee must have cut it out. Bible-study included stories from both the Old and the New Testament, and also 'Catechism' (Q. 'Who made you?' A. 'God'. Q.

14

'Who is God?' A. 'God is a spirit that always was and always will be'. And so on.) Then back to 'Onward, Christian soldiers'. The piano was played by 'Juicy' Hall, aged about thirty, with a blue three-piece suit and black brilliantined hair carefully parted and brushed. As the Sunday school teacher prayed, Juicy would reverently double over on the piano stool, but apparently he didn't always shut his eyes; for once or twice, when he spotted some of us gazing around the room and grinning, he muttered 'Get your heads down!' Seven years or so later, I heard he had just managed to escape from Paris on a push-bike before the Germans arrived. One had a vision of Juicy, keeping his shining head well down as he pedalled furiously for the Channel ports. But what on earth was he doing in Paris?

The Church Hall was the venue of the annual sale of work, which meant scrumptious teas, balloons, and a lot of excited children charging around. I once bought a beautiful necklace for my mother, with big black-and-cream-coloured beads. Twenty years later, when she was near to death and we were sorting out some of her belongings, we came on the necklace. I held it up. 'Yes,' she said. 'Isn't it hideous?' And hideous it undoubtedly was. 'Why on earth didn't you throw it out?' I said. 'Oh no, I couldn't do that. It was the first present you gave me.' At the sale, mother always ran the cake stall with Miss Dorrie Daly, a lady whose frail, ultra-feminine persona was rather deceptive. She surprised me one day by showing up at our house at the wheel of a huge maroon Armstrong-Siddeley with a glittering chromium grille. (None of the women in our connection could drive.) She had come to take Grandpa out for the afternoon. Dorrie Daly also made delicious fudge – absolutely stiff with calories – for which the recipe is: 1lb granulated sugar; $1/4$lb brown cooking sugar; 2oz butter; small half cup of water; a quantity of condensed milk (about two-thirds of a modern tin); bring to the boil, stirring all the time; boil for 15 minutes or so until the mixture becomes bubbly; then pour into greased tins. Dorrie Daly would sometimes add nuts and raisins; but I always regarded that as slightly decadent.

Dorrie's sister, Miss Edie, taught piano to Joan and myself and a number of our friends in a small annexe at the back of her house in Haddon Road. She would sit beside us, exhorting and chiding, as we blundered through Czerny's studies on her battered upright. When it was clear that I had not done my daily half-hour's practice, she would say 'Now you must keep *at* it. Just think how nice it will be to play for people at rugby dinners', from which I inferred that she did not envisage a career for me on the concert platform. On two or three occasions I was sent in for some kind of exam at the Royal Irish Academy of Music in Westland Row. The first time she said, 'You'll have Maestro Viani. He's *very* distinguished, you know.' This caused some apprehension. How could I play in such company, and how could I cope with a grand piano? In the event, Maestro Viani was kind and charming, and issued whatever certificate was necessary. (Did anyone ever fail?) After the first visit, Miss Edie said 'Well, did you enjoy the piano? Was it a Steinway or a Bechstein?' 'Oh no,' I said, 'it was a terrible old thing.' Then, with a gesture, 'almost as bad as...' However, she can't have held it against me, for one evening (probably in 1938) she took me into town as a treat to hear a talk by Mr Ferriss, an Englishman, on the message of the British Israelites. This turned out to be a very fluent performance, drawing on the Old Testament, Revelation, Josephus, and the dimensions of the Great Pyramid. I went to bed trembling at the discovery that the people I had thought of as English, Scottish, Welsh and Irish were actually the lost ten tribes of Israel. More disconcerting still, the Bible showed, when properly interpreted, that Armageddon was not far away; it would all be over by 1957. That gave me less than twenty years to get ready.

Associated with the Methodist church was a troop of scouts, complete with Guides, Cubs and Brownies. But the word which came via my mother from the Poldens was that, although nice people, the Scouts were a slack, undisciplined lot. What was the point of tying knots and lighting fires if you couldn't stand up straight or march in step? The two Polden boys and their sister were in the Boys' and Girls' Brigade, which operated in the Presbyterian church on the corner of Howth Road. So it was decided that I should join the Lifeboys. The uniform (dark blue jersey, large brass badge, and sailors' hat) implied a link with the navy, which was not made explicit but was nevertheless confirmed by the hymn,

Will your anchor hold
In the storms of life,
When the clouds unfold
Their wings of strife?
When the strong tides lift
And the cables strain,
Will your anchor shift
Or firm remain?

A splendid verse. Once a week I reported to the Presbyterian
Church Hall, where the company fell in, marched, and drilled,
then changed for gym, and finally sang a hymn before being dis-
missed. The whole thing was presided over by Miss Muriel Freeman, trim, straight, and strikingly handsome in her long blue coat,
three-cornered hat, and white gloves. One didn't fool around with
Miss Freeman. Eventually the Lifeboys would pass into the Boys'
Brigade, which did the same sort of thing, but had in addition a
deafening bugle band with drums. In retrospect, the Lifeboys and
BB were (and presumably still are) quasi-military organizations.
Yet they were entirely innocent. There were no enemies and
hence no weapons or fighting. One simply learned to act in unison
with others in obeying orders. How useful that is in peacetime is a
matter of opinion; but no doubt the exercises on horse and mat did
us good. There was no denominational dimension. We never
asked or cared who was Methodist, or Presbyterian, or Church of
Ireland. Yet in the outside world in regard to Catholics one was
vaguely aware of a difference. In the bus or tram, men raised their
hats and women crossed themselves when passing St Anthony's
Chapel. That was where Maggie went for mass and confession,
where they said 'Hail Marys' (whatever *they* were) and were told to
do penance. What were they up to? And why were they allowed to
play football on a Sunday? The sad thing was that this slight feeling of constraint discouraged me from asking questions. Similarly,
of all the Catholic children that I knew, none ever asked me about
religion.

My father's people came from Roscrea in Co. Tipperary. Members of the family were there at least as early as the eighteenth century, and at some stage they became millers. My great-grandfa-
ther, who died in 1888, and is buried in St Cronan's churchyard,

was from Abbey Mills, and that is where my grandfather lived until the mill was sold in 1920. At some stage the latter must have left the Church of Ireland, for he is mentioned as Circuit Steward of the Methodist church in 1902 and 1903. That church, a neat and attractive building, also contains a marble tablet commemorating my uncle, who was killed in 1916. My father's early schooldays were spent in Roscrea. Later he boarded, with his older brother, at Wesley College, Dublin; and I never heard him say a good word for it. In this one respect he was like G.B. Shaw. (The headmaster, Dr T.J. Irwin, known to his charges as 'The Devil', was once heard to say in public 'We are not very proud of Shaw'. But as was quickly pointed out, that was probably because Shaw was not very proud of *us*.) On leaving school my father was apprenticed as a motor mechanic, and was eventually set up with a garage and car sales establishment in Dominick Street in central Dublin. His family had by now left Roscrea and were living in Haddon Road. His mother was a small, determined woman who always wore black. It was doubtless on her prompting that he paid court to my mother, who was twelve years his senior and had by now decided not to marry. When she turned him down, Mrs Rudd came round and persuaded her, disastrously, that he was a wild simple lad who just needed the love of a good woman to keep him on the straight and narrow. This was a clever argument, as it appealed to my mother's missionary instincts. Here was a young man whom, with God's help, she might perhaps reform. Alas, it never turned out like that, and the marriage brought untold misery to both of them.

During the 1930s, then, my father made his living in the motor business. When he had taken a car in part exchange he would drive it out to Clontarf to test it. So every week there was a different vehicle outside the door. A bull-nose Morris, a red two-seater Rover with 'dickey', an Overland Whippet, a Morris Cowley, an Alfa Romeo – the variety was endless; but the car he kept for himself was a large Essex Terraplane. As a result of his interest in cars, I was taught the basics of driving at the age of seven or eight. This eccentric feat was possible, because we lived not far from Bull Island, a long, thin finger of land running about three hundred yards offshore from Dollymount to Sutton. The core of the island was occupied by two golf clubs – the Royal Dublin (a somewhat pretentious mock-Tudor edifice which later burned down) and, at the farther end, the smaller and less fashionable St Anne's. Beyond the limits of the links were wild hares, nests with plovers' eggs, and the whistle of curlew. There was no road to St Anne's. One simply drove along the beach. The tide rarely came up high enough to cause problems, and when it went out it left a huge expanse of empty sand for the novice to practise on. Of course I couldn't reach the pedals, but I sat on my father's knee and steered; and when he let out the clutch I would change gear. It was all very enjoyable. Later I found it was done partly to prevent me from getting hooked on motorbikes. These he regarded as criminally dangerous; and since he had injured himself quite badly on some of the early bone-shakers, he was determined that I should not do the same.

One Sunday afternoon (presumably to neutralize the influence of my suit) we drove to Phoenix Park to watch an air display from a back road. A two-seater biplane was going through its routine when suddenly it faltered and began to spin. Down and down it came, hopelessly out of control, until it hit the ground with a sickening crash. As the crowd ran forward in an attempt to rescue the crew (both of whom were killed), my father drove quietly away. He tried to reassure me by saying that people went in for all kinds of weird stunts these days in connection with the film industry. I said nothing, but I wasn't fooled. Phoenix Park was also the scene of pre-war motor racing. I missed the Mercedes and Auto-Union teams (though I carefully collected them on cigarette cards); but the ERA's and Rileys were sufficiently loud and frightening. Again, I was too late for Nuovelari and Carraciola; but I did see Bira, the small Burmese prince, hurtling past in his powerful blue car. A very different outing was the Veteran Car Run which, in 1937 or 38, started from the barracks in Phoenix Park and (in most cases) completed a circuit in Co. Wicklow. My father had somehow dug up an old khaki-coloured de Dion Bouton of 1901 and had got it to go. A friend of his, who worked as a make-up assistant at the Abbey Theatre, supplied them with drooping moustaches and Dundreary whiskers; so off they went, my father wearing a loud check suit and a deer-stalker, his passenger in frock coat and topper. I followed behind in another car with the senior mechanic from the garage. At the end there was a lot of noise and laughter from people in colourful costumes; but it was clear that what gave the most pleasure was all the tinkering and tuning that took place in the preceding weeks, plus the challenge of keeping the things in motion. The actual transit from A to B was slow and precarious. The de Dion never exceeded 20mph, and often needed roadside repairs; its engine capacity was probably about the same as a modern scooter's.

Another outing was a visit to the Metropolitan Hall to see Barna, the great Hungarian, and two of his compatriots, Zabados and Bellak, play table tennis. Zabados was a stout defensive player, who made extraordinary chopped returns from yards behind the table; but even he could not withstand the lightning backhand flick which was Barna's speciality. Our interest in table tennis came from the fact that my father would take me down to the Clontarf Yacht and Boat Club (referred to by my mother as the Clontarf Yacht and Booze Club). We would play there until about 6.45, when the members would begin to drift in. Then I would be driven back to do my homework; my father would return to the club until after midnight. From time to time I would join him for lunch in town. He never went to a restaurant in Grafton Street (like Mitchell's or Bewleys) as my mother would have done. He always took me to Jack Nugent's pub in Essex Street, on the corner before the Dolphin Hotel, which was in fact under the same management. There I would meet his business pals – hearty, decent, pint-swilling men, with whom my mother would have felt slightly uneasy (and they with her). Even if I had been of age, I would then have declined the Guinness or the Power's Gold Label, for I had developed feelings of apprehension about booze. But there was no denying that a plateful of prime roast beef and two veg for 2/6 was excellent value.

For most of the 30s my father belonged to a group which rented shooting rights on one of the Wicklow mountains. So 12-bore shotguns, big leather gun-cases, boxes of cartridges, game-bags, and copies of *The Shooting Times* were regular items of furniture. We also had a succession of four pointers – gentle and affectionate animals, which provided excellent company for a child. As a consequence of all this, at irregular intervals dead game would be brought into the house – pheasants, grouse, partridges, and even the occasional goose, all of which used to hang on the back of the pantry door, before being plucked and gutted and cooked. At that time, too, I was shown how to skin a rabbit – a messy and smelly operation. This interest in blood sports helps to explain the presence of the rifle which nearly put paid to Maggie Gannon. Although he would walk for recreation on mountain or golf-course, my father travelled everywhere else by car. He was experienced and highly expert behind the wheel; but he drove alarmingly fast and was embarrassingly aggressive. When displeased, he would wind down the window and swear at the offending party. This would bring appalled remonstrances from my mother in the back. '*Really*, Sam! *Do* mind your language!' But it never made much difference. This verbal aggressiveness (plus his interest in dogs) was partly responsible for one of my humiliations at school. Miss McKittrick once shrieked in horror, 'Niall! How *dare* you say such a thing!' Miss Florence enquired what was wrong. 'Niall has just called Hamish an ill-bred cur!'

The difference between my parents can be illustrated by a trivial example. Snow had fallen, and my father and I were going out the gate. A woman, who was a total stranger, was coming along the footpath. As she went by, I bent down, scooped up enough snow for a fair-sized ball, and flung it at her retreating figure. She turned and began to protest. At this point my mother would have apologized to the woman and reprimanded me for my bad manners. But my father said, 'Dammit ma'am, were you never young yourself?' This contrast in attitude was apparent in many ways. He was unpunctual, procrastinating, and careless about paying (and collecting) debts. He smoked, drank, swore, and took little interest in his appearance. Someone was once heard to say, 'Does Sam Rudd never wear anything but those damned plus-fours?' This struck a sympathetic chord, and thereafter he was frequently referred to as 'Fours' or 'D.P. Fours'. His virtues are most easily summarized in negative terms. He was free of bigotry, and in later life he reserved his most withering scorn for pharisaical Protestants. He took a low-key attitude to sex. If, for instance, he heard of an unmarried girl becoming pregnant, he would make some comment about the couple's folly rather than their immorality. Adultery or alcoholism would be ascribed to misfortune. Of his own marital troubles he was almost invariably reticent. He would simply say, 'You'll understand it all when you grow up.' Finally, he was indifferent to matters of class. Some of his friends were regarded by my mother as raffish or, as she would say, 'undesirable'. On the other hand his shooting brought him into touch with some well-to-do people, and it would never have occurred to him to make conversational capital out of them. The same applied to public celebrities. Once, quite by accident, I discovered that he knew Yeats. He was speaking of a group who had met in the poet's house in Rathfarnham – not to discuss modern verse, but to witness the psychic powers of the fashionable medium, Mrs Duncan. All he said was that the *séance* had been a flop and that Mrs D. wasn't even good-looking.

I mention this last point, because already then, though to a much greater extent after the war, anyone who could boast of knowing Yeats or Joyce could be sure of free drinks in Davy Byrne's off Grafton Street. There was a story of one leprechaun who used to accost American graduate students. 'So you're doin' a teesis on Joyce, eh?' 'Yes sir, I am. What can I get you to drink?' 'A drop of Jameson's would do nicely.' Half an hour later the conversation would still be in progress. '...and I sez to Joyce, I sez Jim, dis bloody place is banjaxed altogether. Why don't you get out to hell? In fact one day I went further. I said Look at here, Jim, take a tip from me. Go and forge in the smithy of your soul the uncreated conscience of your race.' 'Rillay? You said *that*?' 'Well, wasn't it the good advice? Ah, the same again please, and good luck to ya!'

By 1936 it was time to leave Miss McKittrick's. My father would not allow me to go to Wesley, where The Devil was nearing the end of his long career. But he did agree that I should go to High School, probably not because of Yeats but because the TT motor-cyclist, Stanley Woods, whom he also knew, was a fairly recent old boy. High School was a red-brick building near the top of Harcourt Street. The headmaster was Mr (later Dr) John Bennett, a small top-heavy man with a large scholarly skull, a pair of gold-rimmed glasses, and a chin that disappeared into a high stiff collar. He was known, somewhat unconvincingly, as 'The Bear' or, subsequently, 'Jasper'. The story was that, if you showed any promise in languages, the Bear would seize you at the age of fifteen and coach you in Classics for a sizarship (an entrance scholarship to Trinity College). If you were any good at numbers, Victor Graham, a young and very talented teacher, would do the same for you in Maths. Because of those two men, and one or two others, the school had a good academic reputation, at least in certain areas.

More formidable, however, than any member of staff was Sergeant 'Frosty' Nelson who had a cubby-hole with a tall desk just inside the front door. Frosty was a small, compact Scot, now in his early seventies, with fierce eyebrows and a white moustache, who wore the navy-blue uniform of the eleventh Hussars, complete with medal ribbons. He showed no respect whatever for the teaching staff. Every morning he would make a noisy entrance and come clumping up the wooden floor in his army boots. The teacher had to break off, while Frosty, glaring over his glasses, said 'How many of yeez buys is takin' dinner today?' A similar round took place in the afternoon, when Frosty would read out the detention list. The only protest at his behaviour came from the Vicar who taught Scripture. Speaking to one of the class, he said 'My dear fellow, don't call the Sergeant Sir. He may be a splendid chap, but he's only the janitor, you know'. But our awe was undiminished. Once, when passing the Sergeant's empty office, I saw my water-pistol lying on his desk. It was the best I ever had, firing six drenching jets in quick succession; and it had been confiscated in the first week of its use. Yet I was too scared to nip in and recover it. The central position which he occupied in the boys' mind was shown by the end-of-term chant:

> This time next week where will I be?
> Far from the gates of HSD.
> Kick up tables, kick up chairs,
> Kick old Frosty down the stairs.

French was taught by H.R. Chillingworth, a gentleman of the old school. He was a large portly man with a smooth pink face and silky white hair. Perversely, I recall almost nothing of his teaching,

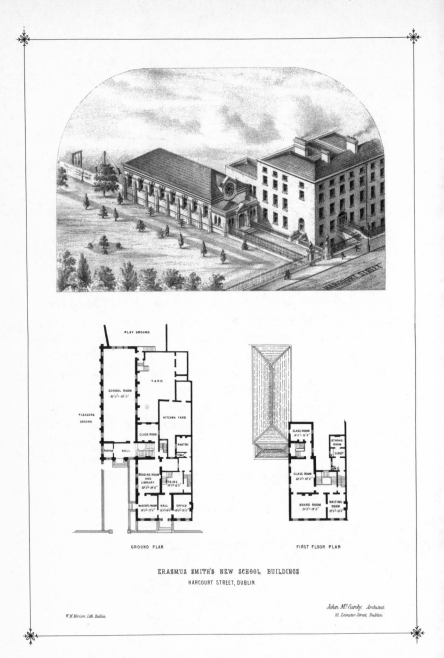

The High School, Dublin (architect's plan and elevation), *c.* 1870.

except for a moving account of the death of Socrates. The most interesting thing about his room was the ceiling. Since it had last been painted (and when was that?) a long succession of schoolboys had moistened coloured blotting paper in their mouths, fitted the sodden ball onto the end of a ruler, and then, when Chillingworth turned to the blackboard, flipped the pellet up to the ceiling, where it stuck with a soft plop. The result was a variegated, three-dimensional, surface which looked as if it had been applied by a crazy stuccoer.

In charge of art and woodwork was a genial Ulsterman, Mr Wilson. A slightly weird-looking character with wisps of hair falling onto his shoulders, he was reputedly interested in spiritual-ism. Apart from painting the set for the school's annual production of Gilbert and Sullivan (which he did very well), he just sat by his stove, chatting to anyone who dropped in. After telling us to open our folios, he would make no attempt whatever to teach us draw-ing. As with Chillingworth's description of the death of Socrates, the only lesson of Wilson's that I remember was a disquisition on home-grown tomatoes.

'The quality of mercy is not strain'd./It droppeth as the gentle rain from heaven/Upon the place beneath...' The speech stays in my mind after more than half a century; and having seen rote-learning pass out of fashion (with the consequent atrophy of the memory) I am less inclined than I once was to decry the practice. Nevertheless, Shakespeare was just too hard for ten-year-olds. Or if we *were* going to study *The Merchant of Venice*, we should have been given some elementary help. (To this day I am still not sure of what is meant by 'strain'd' in Portia's famous lines.) But Boozy Butler either overestimated our ability or else was unaware of the problems. He had strange hair – a kind of dull brass, fading to white around the edges. It could hardly have been a wig, because it was matched by his moustache, which stood out against a mottled crimson face. He wore a suit of pepper-and-salt plus-fours, and stood very erect, which gave him the appearance of a retired colonel. Comical as it now seems, he used to speak in his clipped Anglo-Irish voice about 'keeping a straight bat'. But the ethics of cricket must have become adulterated with commercialism. For when a boy committed some minor offence he would bark 'You little cad! They don't want that kind of thing in Guinness's!' If the misdemeanour was more serious, he would line up three boys against the wall, stare at one who was innocent, and, while berating him, flash out and catch the guilty boy a slap in the face. Then the class would resume, as somebody recited 'The Wreck of the Hesperus' or 'Lord Ullin's Daughter'.

Occasionally Mr Butler, who belonged to that distinguished Anglo-Irish family, would tell stories. One was about a British spy in France during the first world war. 'After sending back a lot of information by carrier pigeon, the man was caught by the Germans. To maintain his cover he decided to pose as a lunatic, and he kept this up during his interrogation so successfully that the Germans were almost taken in.' (At this point Boozy began to stalk around the room, staring at the ceiling, and swaying from side to side. The class was impressed, given that this was an Irish schoolmaster in Dublin imitating an English spy imitating a half-witted French peasant.) 'But just before they let him go, they examined his jacket once again and discovered a grain of wheat in one of the pockets. That did it. Next day the poor fellow was shot at dawn.' Then, noticing stupid faces all round, he added 'Don't you see, dammit? The Hun knew he had been feeding pigeons!'

Inspectors occasionally visited the school. Once our singing class was subjected to a sort of mass oral, in which one question seemed especially foul. 'What is the difference between *rallentando* and *ritardando*?' I glanced at our teacher in some bewilderment, as I didn't know there *was* any difference; but his face wore a faint, sphinx-like smile. So I kept quiet. At last a red-haired chap called Burgess, who had the instincts of a gambler, said, 'Sir, I believe *rallentando* is a rather slower form of *ritardando*.' Nice try. Another day an inspector came into our Irish class, which was taken at that time by a part-time teacher. We had been drilled in a few simple responses to a given set of questions. Unfortunately when the teacher put the first question he forgot the name of the boy whom he wanted to answer; he simply said 'Yo'. All very well, but as the man happened to have a ferocious squint two other boys thought he was looking at them. The result was an answer by three voices in unison, which rather spoiled the effect of spontaneity. One of the poems I learned that term was Dr Douglas Hyde's 'In the glen where I was born'. The sad thing is that I remember the Irish well enough, but have no idea what it means – an experience familiar to any ageing parrot.

In those three years (1936–9) my friends and I began to read periodicals like *The Skipper*, *The Rover*, *The Hotspur*, and *The Adventure*. One exciting serial was called 'Gunsmoke Rides at Midnight'; its hero was one Lefty Clavering who was unbelievably fast on the draw. Another was 'The Lost Galleon', the tale of a crew who had somehow got lost in time and had survived until the present day, mouthing strange archaisms ('Ho there, varlet!') and still wearing their Tudor clobber. Most remarkable of all was 'The Wolf of Kabul', who caused mayhem in the Khyber Pass with no weapon other than a well-seasoned cricket bat. I think affectionately of those stories, since they were the first things that I read for myself with real excitement.

If reading counts as a sign of approaching maturity, another memory points backwards. Though Peter Comley and I were driven to school by my father at a furious speed, arriving with nerves taut just as the bell sounded, we would often make our way home separately, taking the tram down Harcourt Street and Dawson Street to O'Connell Bridge, and then hurrying down Eden Quay to catch the new green double-decker bus to Clontarf. Two parallel sets of lines ran across O'Connell Bridge, leaving about three feet between the trams as they passed in opposite directions. At some point I formed the lunatic habit of alighting from the tram, counting one two three, and charging across the other track without looking. Sometimes, of course, there was no oncoming tram to be seen; sometimes it was in sight, but more than twenty yards away. But once, as I played this game of tramcar roulette, I came within a whisker of being mown down. I got such a fright that I fled across the bridge without daring to look back, pursued by the sound of the tram's bell as the driver stamped on it in fury.

The trams started from Nelson's Pillar. As one always ignores what is most familiar, I did not climb the Pillar until prodded into doing so by a visitor. On emerging from the dark spiral staircase, I inched around the top on hands and knees, afraid to look over the parapet. Some years later, after a few spectacular and messy suicides, they enclosed the platform in an unsightly wire cage. No doubt the black-shawled women at the fruit-stalls underneath ('Penny each o'bananas!') were much relieved. On special occasions my cousin Joan and I were taken up Henry Street to Arnotts. I have suppressed all disagreeable memories of trying on clothes, but I do recall how the shop assistants would put the money into a six-inch cylinder, pull a lever, and with a metallic plop send the cylinder speeding along an overhead wire to the cashier's box. Todd Byrne's, farther up the street, was better still; for they had 'the dodgems'. Whoever invented the name totally misunderstood their function, for the real object of driving the cars was to bash into as many people as possible.

To get to Arnotts and Todd Byrne's, one had to pass the end of Moore Street with its colourful market; we were never taken down it. There were large stores, too, where we never went. As I was massively incurious about shopping, I did not ask why. But retrospect suggests an unstated system of 'yes's' and 'no's'. There were Switzers and Brown Thomas's (yes), and Clerys and Guineys (no). The system extended further. So one had *The Irish Times* (yes), and the *Irish Press* (no). The Metropole, Capital and Savoy cinemas (yes), and the Corinthian (no). The Gaiety Theatre (yes), and the Olympia (no). The system, as I say, was unstated; it may not even have been consciously formulated. But it must have been based on a mixture of politics, religion, and class. *The Irish Times* was Protestant and pro-British, while the *Irish Press* was Catholic and republican. The *Irish Independent* lay somewhere in between, but was probably more 'no' than 'yes'. (Once, in the 1950s, my cousin Buddy Polden bet a business colleague that there would be a photo of a priest in the *Independent* every day for a week. He duly collected.) We were too young for the theatre; but the Christmas pantomime at the Gaiety would be some wholesome production like Peter Pan, with an English lady (Ivy Tresman) in the leading role, whereas Jimmy O'Dea, who according to my mother had a thick Dublin accent and was notoriously vulgar, was always at the Olympia. Again, the OK cinemas showed films like *The Four Feathers*, *The Lives of a Bengal Lancer*, *Gunga Din*, and *The Drum* – i.e. imperialistic nostalgia, whereas the Corinthian went in for gangsterdom and the wild west. (It was known to its devotees as *The Ranch*.) As for comedy, like everyone else of my age, I was paralysed with laughter by Laurel and Hardy and the Three Stooges; but, embarrassingly, I was one of those who found Chaplin neither funny nor pathetic but merely a bore.

This pattern of respectability, which was in the main associated with my mother and her sister (Aunt Connie), was sometimes broken by my father. For example, he took me to see the wrestler Dan O'Mahony, who demonstrated his special throw ('The Irish whip') on some luckless stooge engaged for the purpose. Later, Dad must have met Danno at a dinner party; for he brought me the great man's signature on a menu card. Then there was the magician Levant (sometimes paired with the equally famous Maskelyne). Levant's *pièce de résistance* was to pour endless pints of Guinness out of a small kettle and hand them round the audience. At the end, in an atmosphere of uproarious jollity, he gave away the magic receptacle to an eager member of the audience, who found, of course, that it was just an ordinary tin kettle. I do not know what Levant did during the war; but Maskelyne was much in demand as an expert in camouflage.

Visits to the zoo in Phoenix Park were organized by my mother and aunts. On passing through a turnstile in a thatched cottage, one turned right, making for the zoo's buildings and passing the bisons' enclosure in the corner. Those huge wedge-shaped monsters always looked untidy, as if someone had taken a thick, dirty-yellow, rug and flung it over their backs. It was hard to associate such sad apathetic creatures with the herds that stampeded across the prairies. The lion-house was memorable for the pungent stench that hit you as you went through the door. It was advisable to be there a few minutes before feeding time; for then the lions and tigers would be pacing to and fro and roaring with hunger. Suddenly a door would clang open at the far end of the building and a large iron cart would be wheeled in, piled with carcasses of raw meat. The keeper would then spear a lump of meat with a long two-pronged fork and thrust it through an aperture below the bars, from where it would be seized by a pair of savage claws and dragged inside. Even to a ten-year-old, however, the whole set-up seemed cruelly unnatural. A few years later things improved when the big cats were freed from those horrible cages and put into an enclosure on the far side of the gardens. But why have them at all?

In those days it was argued that they served an educational purpose, that otherwise children would never know what they were really like. At the end of the century, however, that argument hardly holds, for almost every week one sees the most wonderful films of animals in their natural habitat. The other argument, namely that the big cats' survival depends on the breeding carried out in western zoos, seems somewhat disingenuous. How many tigers, one wonders, have been restored to the wild from the Phoenix Park?

Such problems became less obvious as we ran on to the monkey house. Feeding was permitted, and here my father had given me a useful tip: 'Don't bother about monkey-nuts; take a few scallions with you. The monkeys love them.' So we brought along handfuls of scallions (which in England are usually called spring onions); and it was quite true. Even the most listless old chimpanzees would become animated at the smell of those little white bulbs. In adjoining cages chattering brawls would develop as the smaller monkeys grabbed the green shoots and carried them up to the topmost perches. Then they would come swinging down again, pushing their black fingers through the bars for another pungent treat. The reptile house with its clammy equatorial atmosphere was quite exciting, but never wholly fulfilled its promise. One knew, for example, that a python could open its jaws wider and wider and slowly engulf a sheep. But this never happened. One did not even see an interesting bulge in the great reptile's stomach – just a heap of motionless coils. Then there was the crocodile, the terror of the African river-banks, which could amputate a leg with one snap of its terrible jaws. But how could that reputation be squared with the comatose creature lying in a sunken bath in the middle of the floor? The keeper once told me that if I tried to join it in the bath it would soon wake up; but, like most theorizing, that remained unsatisfactory. Such objections applied less to the elephants, which took children for slow ponderous rides along the tarmac road; still, the great intelligence which the elephant was said to possess did not seem to be fully displayed by taking a battered tin plate from a visitor's hand and delivering it to the keeper to be refilled with lumps of stale bread. Much better, and perhaps indeed as good as the monkeys, were the sea-lions. Sleek and elegant, they gave every appearance of enjoying their tricks as they caught fish in mid-air or dived for it in the depths of the pool. Yet, although it was fun to see them in the flesh, they too were in a sadly confined space. (Did they dream of the Gulf of California?) In all these cases, perhaps the best compromise for the time being is the wild-life park.

Visits to the zoo took place only once or twice a year. Sport was a more frequent source of entertainment. By the mid-30s 'the wireless', as we called it, was broadcasting exciting commentaries on Wimbledon. My mother and I listened eagerly to the epic struggles of Perry, Cochet, Budge and Von Kramm, and to the even faster exchanges of Perry and Austin, Borotra and Brugnon, Crawford and Quist. When there were special events at the Fitz-william Club, we went to watch. In that way we saw the Davis Cup match between Ireland and Sweden. The two most individual players were G. Lyttleton-Rogers, a tall angular man with sharp nose and thinning hair whose knees were covered by a pair of cream-coloured shorts, and the blond-haired and glamorous Lester Sto-fen, who wore the more conventional slacks. That was all good stuff; but richer fare was provided by the visits of Tilden, Budge, Cochet, and Vines. The dark, olive-skinned Cochet was a relatively short man, but agile and well balanced and a highly accurate volleyer. Ellsworth Vines was especially strong on the backhand. The red-haired Budge was at this time the best all-round player in the world. But the most remarkable figure was undoubtedly Big Bill Tilden, who had won Wimbledon for the third time in 1930. Such a celebrity did not have to wear ordinary clothes. He appeared in a royal blue, half-sleeve, shirt of a strange velvety material. His racket was not only without a grip; it also had a triangular hole at the shoulders where it should (one would have thought) have been strongest. Add a pair of very long white trousers, and place on top of everything the head of a refined chimpanzee, and the result was the most famous tennis personality of the inter-war years. Much later, one's belief in stereotypes was jolted by reports that he had been involved in some kind of homosexual scandal.

Tennis, at club level, also took place in Clontarf; but I was too young to participate. There were other things to do. The boat club had much to interest a youngster of ten or eleven. When the tide was out, the boats lay on their sides on the grey mud looking stricken and helpless. But as the water came in they would slowly resume their dignity, and ride serenely at their moorings – May Mischief (scarlet), Crusader (white), Ranger (yellow), Murrumbidgee (black), and a score of others. A wooden slipway ran out from the sea wall, and those without dinghies would be rowed to their boats by Bill Bassett, a small wiry old man with a brown weather-beaten face and a white moustache. He wore a yachting cap, a navy-blue jersey with the club's initials (CYBC) embroidered in red, blue trousers, and a pair of rubber boots. He was rude and cantankerous to all alike, adopting the persona of 'the old salt'. But as he had been there so long no one dared to tell him off. I was careful to stay out of his way. When the cannon was fired, and a race got under way, the boats would first sail parallel to the sea front, then head out towards the two lighthouses that marked the entrance to the Liffey. Rounding a buoy, they would make up river and then come round in a big sweep to the finishing-line. As they were a miscellaneous collection, there was a careful system of handicaps. Without that, Derek Luke's Murrumbidgee, a clinker-built boat with high mast and bermuda rig from the yard of the Dublin shipwright Carney, would have won every race. In time, some fourteen-foot international dinghies and a few Fireflies ap-peared; these would compete in class races at regattas in Howth and Dún Laoghaire.

In the saloon of the Boat Club there was an attractive portrait by Gerald Bruen of a local character called Christy Swords. The old fellow was shown sitting on the sea wall wearing a high felt hat and fawn-coloured trousers. His legs were crossed, and he held a pipe in one hand and a box of matches in the other. My mother must have admired the picture, because Dad persuaded the artist to do a copy, which he brought home to Lissadell. There was a slight contretemps when my Uncle Herbert (Stan Polden's brother) enquired whether it was an advertisement for Friendly Matches. My father at once took it back to the artist and asked him to make the lettering on the matchbox a little less distinct. The picture remained in Lissadell until 1938, when old James Cooke died and we left the house.

Moving along the sea front from the Bull Island towards the city one passed Peter Comley's house, which proclaimed its modernity by having a flat roof, wide metal-framed windows, and white concrete walls. Then came the Boat Club, set well back from the road, with a flagpole on the grass in front of it, and then the white-washed structure of Clontarf baths. Here mixed bathing was forbidden; on entry one turned left or right – a reminder that Victorian prudery was not confined to Protestants. I don't know if women bathed there all the year round, but some men certainly did; for there was a swim every Christmas morning, and on the wall of the changing-room there was a photo of a bravely smiling group who had on one occasion literally broken the ice. Even in summer I found it paralysingly cold. Blackrock baths on the other side of the bay were no better. That was where my cousin Joan and I were taught to swim by Mr Case, who made absolute beginners lie on a canvas loop at the end of a bamboo pole while they did a frantic breaststroke, eyes closed and head in air. Then they graduated to a lifebelt improvised out of an inflated bicycle tube. And finally they struck out on their own, moving slowly across a corner of the shallow end. I had just reached this last stage when our lessons were transferred to the indoor baths in Tara Street, where the air smelt damp and chlorinated, but the pool itself was bearable in temperature, though noticeably less buoyant. On the first day, I set off across a corner of the deep end. On reaching the edge I grabbed for the rail, missed, and began to sink. Mr Case and his bamboo pole were far away, but luckily Aunt Connie saw what had happened, knelt down in her lisle stockings on the wet surround, and thrust the handle of her umbrella below the surface. With a last desperate effort I clutched it and was hauled to safety. It must have felt like a close call, for I lay shuddering and gasping at the pool-side for some minutes, before hurrying away to get dressed. Afterwards wise people told me I should have dived in again to recover my nerve. No doubt they were right, but it was weeks before I returned to the pool, and then I made sure to start again at the shallow end.

On the right hand side of Castle Avenue, a hundred yards or so from the sea, a lion poked its head through the wall and spewed water into a small stone basin. This, Brian Boru's Well, commemorated the Battle of Clontarf, where on Good Friday 1014 Brian's army dispelled the threat of Scandinavian supremacy. It sounds

like a fairly typical achievement, for apart from removing the Nor-
semen, 'the main result of the battle of Clontarf was to weaken the
central power and to throw the whole island into a state of anarchy' (*Encyclopedia Brittanica*, edn 11, vol.14, 766–7). Two hundred
yards or so beyond the wall, the road skirted Clontarf Castle and
eventually passed an imposing iron gateway on the left which gave
access to the Clontarf Cricket and Football Club. On Saturday
afternoons in the summer I used to get in free by undertaking to
work the scoreboard, which simply meant hooking black metal
squares, painted with white numbers, onto a board outside the
pavilion. Tom Sweeney scorned this stratagem, preferring to
install himself in a tree in a laneway which ran alongside the
ground. From our separate vantage points we would watch the
exploits of players like Boucher (Phoenix) and Ingram (Leinster).
These were two of the best cricketers in the country, and it was
mortifying to be told that they would be lucky to make one of the
weaker county teams in England. About 1938 Tommy Headon
appeared in the middle of Clontarf's batting order. He did not
relish sprinting between the wickets, but as he had an excellent eye
he was able to score most of his runs from boundaries. Once in the
early years of the war he told me he was in trouble with the club
for losing so many balls, and it is true that he would often jump
out of his crease and send the ball soaring across the road into the
grounds of Blackheath (now an orthopaedic hospital).

   In September, when the rugger season began, my grandfather
and my mother, plus all members of the Polden family who were
not actually playing, would attend the first fifteen's matches. S.E.
Polden had joined the club after leaving school, and had represented Ireland at scrum-half in the seasons just before and just after the
first world war. He maintained his connection with the club for
over half a century, even after he had left the district and his sons
had moved to Old Wesley. In 1933, the first season that I remember in any detail, he was President of the Irish Union and one of
the selectors, but that did not affect his work for Clontarf. The
women in the family also contributed in a practical way. On Saturday mornings, when Uncle Stan was still at his desk in the Ballast
Office, Aunt Connie, my mother, and Molly Egan (a daily help
who was unfailingly kind to us all as we grew up) had been at work

in the kitchen of the Poldens' house. Here huge quantities of sand-wiches, and piles of Bewleys' brack were cut and buttered. Sausage rolls and apple pies were added; and then the whole lot was trans-ported to the pavilion where, after the game, it was de-voured by players, officials, and sundry hangers-on. Clontarf was the only local club in Leinster. The others had their grounds closer to the city. This may have accounted for the vociferous support which the team commanded ('come on 'TAARF!'). Elsewhere it was said that any player visiting Clontarf had to be careful not to step out of line, otherwise he might be thrown to the spectators. (I note, incidental-ly, for the sake of economic historians, that the excellent fruit brack mentioned above was made by Bewleys until the late 1980s. The firm which now operates under the same name no longer uses that recipe. Apparently the old-style brack would now cost so much to make that it could no longer be sold at a profit.)

The Clontarf team, in its broad red and blue stripes and white shorts, did quite well in those years, winning the Leinster cup in 1936. The two stars were Fred Moran and George Morgan. Moran was a powerfully built fellow with a rather ungainly style. But he was the Irish sprint champion, and when he burst through the centre no one could get near him. Once, when I was sitting on the rail that ran along the touchline, Fred Moran cannoned into me, squashing my legs painfully underneath the bar. He immedi-ately steadied me and asked if I was all right. I was so overcome with the honour of being injured by Fred Moran that I could only nod, wide-eyed. Moran's father ran a good, moderately priced, hotel in Talbot Street, opposite the Great Northern station. In the course of his job Moran senior had learned to speak French, so he was always in demand as an interpreter when the French team came to Dublin after the war. Fred Moran's aunt, Miss Fran Moran, became Professor of Law at Trinity College, one of the first ladies to hold a Chair.

George Morgan, who worked in the Royal Bank, was the best scrum-half to play for Ireland in the sixty years that I remember. (Older observers used to say that Mark Sugden was equally good.) He had a deceptively lazy manner, and a bland innocent face that gulled many an opponent into buying a dummy. In fact in his first international, against England at Lansdowne Road in 1934, he persuaded the full-back to go for the right wing while he himself slipped over for a try. In 1937, at Twickenham, he gathered the ball from a loose scrum and glanced across to the wing. Fred Moran had already started his sprint for the line, and when Morgan put in the cross kick, he won the race for the touch-down. On that same occasion H.S. Sever, the English wing, made a great run up the line. He was eventually forced into touch, taking the corner flag with him. Uncle Stan, who as touch-judge was standing about a yard from the action, was able to tell the referee that Sever had first grounded the ball for a try. This did not stop some Irish reporters, who were in the press-box in the grandstand on the other side of the field, from complaining that the touch-judge's foolish error had cost Ireland the match (England won by 9 to 8). These remarks caused much indignation at home, but Uncle Stan, whose speech habits were laconic, said, 'Ah, let them go to the mischief! I simply said what I saw.'

As we were a rugby family, Lansdowne Road was a definite 'yes', whereas Dalymount Park (soccer) and Croke Park (hurling) were 'no's', A friend once remarked that in the Polden family rugby was next to God; someone else answered 'I'm not so sure.' In fact, we were fairly typical. The reasons for our devotion were never enunciated, and no doubt it was largely a matter of tradition and habit. Yet, half-consciously, rugby was in part a political choice. For it was not a 'Gaelic game' (and was for that reason shunned by de Valera though he had played it at Blackrock). On the contrary it was a game which looked outwards, and tied the Irish to the United Kingdom and what was still known as 'the Empire'. Ironically, from Dev's point of view, it was also a game in which Ireland competed as one country. The reason for this should perhaps be sought in the fact that the expanding social class that played rugger on each side of the border, and had common interests in business and the professions, took the very sensible view that political and religious quarrels ought not to interfere with something as important as sport. In the late 1940s it was thought to be of only passing interest that an IRA man should be packing in the same scrum as a member of the RUC. In any case, for whatever reason, I absorbed the rugby ethos. It was not until thirty years later, when I had moved to Liverpool, that I attended a first-class soccer match. I have still not seen gaelic or hurling except on television.

Since my father never came with us to Lansdowne Road and Uncle Stan did not drive, we would take a bus to Amiens Street station. (A little farther along, waiting by the ramp of the Great Northern terminus, was a row of black, horse-drawn cabs. The horses would stand there patiently, with sacks thrown over them in cold weather, sometimes munching in their nosebags. They contrasted oddly with the Chryslers and Ford V8's purchased by more up-to-date cab-owners.) On boarding the train on 'the loop line' we crossed the river to Tara Street by a huge iron bridge which effectively blotted out one of Dublin's finest buildings – Gandon's Custom House; then on to Westland Row, and finally to Lansdowne Road, where we left the platform by a small gate and joined the crowd that had walked up the road. On the old stand, up behind the committee box, I would snuggle in amongst the tweeds, rugs, fur coats, and cigar smoke, and wait eagerly for the match to begin, whether it was schools' cup, senior cup, interprovincial, seven-a-side, or provincial town's cup. This last competition was played as a curtain-raiser to the senior cup final. Teams with names like Wexford Wanderers and Shannon Buccaneers (the latter with skull and crossbones emblazoned on a bright red jersey) did battle before a crowd of city spectators who shouted with superior laughter at the antics of their country cousins.

At internationals we sat on benches temporarily erected beside the touchline. As we were always early, there was plenty of time to study the photos and read the programme notes on the players. The heaviest Irish forward from 1933–9 was, I believe, Jack Siggins, who weighed about 16½ stone; all the rest were under 16. Half a century later Willie John MacBride was over 17 stone, and the rest were correspondingly heavier than their predecessors. No doubt this simply reflects a general trend, but perhaps it may also suggest that physical evolution has lost touch with the requirements of survival. Not only was there less weight in those days, there was also less skill. Forwards were not expected to run and pass; it was more a matter of kick and rush – especially with the Irish. There were few forwards like Jack Russell, who though over 15 stone was at the same time a champion hurdler.

As we read the details about the Englishmen Toft, Cranmer, and Owen-Smith (a running full-back before his time), or the Scots Logan, Shaw and Dick, a military band would be playing on the pitch. The appropriateness of this was accepted automatically. After all, a great spectacle of physical endeavour, in which heroes struggled for mastery, bringing fear and exultation to thousands, could hardly have been prefaced by a string quartet. The status of rugby as a surrogate for war was recognized by Blackrock College, the dominant rugby school in Dublin in those years; for when one of their boys was injured, the supporters would break into the chorus 'Old Soldiers never die'. And yet we must remember Dr Johnson (one must *always* remember Dr Johnson). Opposing the view that an audience really succumbs to illusion, believing itself in Cleopatra's Egypt or Hamlet's Elsinore, he says, 'the truth is that the spectators are in their senses'. At a deeper level, of course, they are. The referee is there to insist on the primacy of the game, and one has only to think of the horror that engulfs the community on those extremely rare occasions when a player is actually killed. Yet the element of play is only intermittently acknowledged by those on the field. Instructions are yelled; faces are set in masks of sweaty determination. The only clear exception to this that I can think of was the Irish forward Seamus Deering. Whether playing for Bective, Leinster, or Ireland, he would emerge from the bottom of every ruck, with sleeves rolled up and bald head spattered with mud, grinning in sheer delight. His huge sense of enjoyment communicated itself to the crowd, and he was a favourite with spectators, whatever side they were on.

Suddenly the music had finished. The noise of the crowd rose to a deafening roar, and the teams ran onto the field. One noticed that while the English and Scots dressed uniformly, the Irish wore their club stockings. So each player carried onto the pitch the sign of his local origins. In 1960 this practice was abandoned, and Ireland fell into line. Perhaps it was just a coincidence that about the same time national sides were beginning to achieve a sort of independent status. As the game developed in other countries, representative matches were increasing. The stars appeared less often for their clubs, forming instead a glamorous supranational élite which performed on colour television and brought in huge sums of money; it is no accident that the problem of professionalism should first have arisen in connection with national sides. Meanwhile the structure still rests on the foundation of amateur clubs. One wonders whether enough is being done for their welfare.

In the 1930s, however, such thoughts were far away. Above the stockings, of whatever colour, appeared a pair of pale knees; and two or three inches above those came a pair of white shorts. The length of the shorts may have been influenced by decency as well as warmth; certainly, if they were torn in the rough and tumble, a group of team-mates would cluster round to protect the player's modesty. Pale knees served to distinguish the home unions from the All Blacks, who came to Dublin in 1936, and whose knees and lower thighs were enviably tanned. This tan was associated in my mind with the sunny climate enjoyed by 'colonials' – a word which illustrates the pitfalls of language. In those days (at least to people like me) the word inspired admiration and awe, connected as it was with tall muscular men who won at rugby, rowed in the Oxford eight, and were probably Rhodes scholars as well. Such men were also relations who had rallied to the flag, not only from New Zealand, but from South Africa, Canada, and Australia. It therefore came as a shock to find, many years later, that, with its connotations of youth and tutelage, the word inspired fury in those very countries.

While England, Scotland and New Zealand visited Dublin, one had to go to Belfast to see Wales. I was taken on the trip in 1937 and '39. It was an exciting, all-day affair – up to catch the morning train, across the Boyne on the great viaduct, then on to Belfast, where we lunched at Thompson's restaurant in Donegall Place. This in itself was an event, for my people hardly ever ate in restaurants, any more than they rode in taxis or took continental holidays. Then we struggled onto a tram, surrounded by vociferous Welshmen with red and white rosettes. This was rather alarming for a ten-year-old, especially as I had picked up some garbled report about the menace of a Welsh crowd. 'That's why we don't play them in Dublin, you see. If we did, they'd come across in their thousands and cause a riot. Why, they might even tunnel their way into Lansdowne Road!' The picture of a Welsh phalanx, armed with picks and shovels (and probably singing 'Cwm Rhonda' in full harmony) linked up with another half-baked rumour. 'They're a tough lot, you know, they're all miners.' I reported this last point to Tom Sweeney, who, as so often, put me straight. 'That can't be entirely true. Wooller, for instance, went to Cambridge, and Jenkins to Oxford. And anyhow, even if you are a miner, that doesn't mean you aren't a sport.' At Ravenhill another worry arose: could the players from Southern Ireland be relied on to stand to attention for 'God Save the King'? The Ulstermen had very decently stood for 'The Soldiers' Song' in Dublin, though they couldn't possibly have regarded it as a proper national anthem. In the event all was well, and decorum was preserved. By 1939 these worries had largely evaporated. The main question centred on the game itself. Ireland was said to have good forwards – there were Dave O'Loughlin and Blair Mayne, to say nothing of Tommy Headon whom I admired like an elder brother; whereas Wales, we were told, had a rather inexperienced side. (The record-book shows, in fact, that eight of their players were in their first international season.) Nevertheless, Wales had stalwarts like W.H. Travers and Wilfrid Wooller; and Haydn Tanner was one of the great scrum-halves. So there was no cause for excessive confidence. Wales won by seven points to nil. That was the last international before the war. Six months later Hitler's tanks rolled into Poland.

Ballymoney

In 1929 Ballymoney on the Wexford coast, some sixty miles south of Dublin, was a quiet place. At the Post Office you turned east on a country road. (The only tarred surface was on the main road to Dublin which ran a couple of miles inland.) Passing under a high archway of trees you continued for half a mile before descending into a hollow. Here Connors' white-washed house (Rose Cottage) was on the right, and on the left a stony path sloped down to Cooney's farm, which was hidden from view. Then, on climbing a small rise, you caught your first glimpse of the sea about a quarter of a mile away at the bottom of the hill. There were no houses down there, except for the coastguard station, which was set well back from the road, high on the south side of the valley. It was a long two-storey building with a slate roof, drab stucco walls, and a square pointed tower at the end nearest the sea. The station contained five small houses, built for the coastguards and their families in the nineteenth century. One day, in that summer of 1929, when my uncle, Stan Polden, was spending a holiday in the station (then owned by a Mr Ireton), he looked north across the valley and thought how nice it would be to have a bungalow there. He did his sums, borrowed some money from his brother-in-law (Dr Ernest Cooke), and engaged Jimmy MacDonald, a local builder. A year later a dark-green wooden bungalow with a red corrugated-iron roof and white window-frames stood ready. It had a central living-room, bedrooms at three corners, and a tiny kitchen at the fourth. Out at the back were a tool-shed, a coal-house and a lavatory. The total cost was £300.

There were few amenities. Drinking-water had to be fetched in pails from Cooney's farm, where a small stream came down from Tara Hill. (We used to put a fern-leaf on the top of each pail to stop the water from slopping over the sides. Whether it did any good or not, I never knew.) Rain-water for washing was collected in two large barrels as it ran off the roof. Water for the lavatory was pumped up from the river by a hand pump, which was primed with the aid of a tundish. Light came from paraffin lamps, and cooking was done on a range and two primus stoves. In the early years my mother and Aunt Connie would ride into Gorey, some five miles inland, on two very upright bicycles with tyres an inch and a half wide. The groceries they ordered would then be delivered by cart or van. Later, when his two sons learned to drive, Uncle Stan bought a large maroon Austin, second-hand, from my father; which meant that people could come down at weekends as well as on their holidays. But Joan and I spent ten consecutive weeks there every summer for the next fifteen years, so that the place became a second world, where one heard news of what was happening in the city but for the most part carried on a separate existence. People somehow looked and behaved differently in Ballymoney; there were Ballymoney clothes and games, and even a special kind of Ballymoney boredom. Now, of course, the place has changed. In the sixty years since the bungalow was built, chalets have sprouted on a neighbouring headland, fields have been turned over to mobile homes, and new bungalows have appeared at the roadside. But work has come to what was once a rather depressed area; and if the beauty and character of the place have been sadly impaired (as they have), one has to admit that the first step on the downward path was taken by Stan Polden and his relatives.

In the early thirties, however, none of this had happened. To the south ran a series of beautiful sandy beaches, the last stretching for over a mile from Dodd's Rocks to the sleepy, slightly rundown, fishing village of Courtown. To the north the cliffs were higher, but the beaches were just as fine, running up to Castletown and Kilmichael, just south of Arklow. Inland, slightly to the north, rose Tara Hill, with its bare heathery slopes, dividing the coastal strip from the green patchwork of the Irish hinterland. The road which came down the valley turned left at the beach, crossed a beautifully made stone bridge, and then rounded a headland before petering out on the north shore. Below the bridge the beach was divided by a small stream which came down from Tara and flowed through Cooney's farm. Emerging from under the bridge, it descended through a series of rocky pools where you could catch small eels about two inches long. (The unsubtle technique was to scoop up a handful of gravel and weed and throw the whole lot onto a rock. The eels could then be caught as they tried to wriggle back to the water.) Lower down, because of the varying amount of sand brought in, the stream continually changed its course. Often there would be a pool large enough for sailing toy boats. Once it was so big that we were able to punt around a ramshackle raft made of fishermen's corks and a few spars of wood. If there was no pool, the river could always be dammed. The method, which we assumed was original, was to pile up two towers of sand, one on each bank, and then push them together into the stream, strengthening the bottom of the dam with large flat stones.

Although the normal variations of tide covered no more than twenty yards, the configuration of the beach would change dramatically. Huge mounds of gravel would be dumped overnight; rocks which had been hidden for weeks would suddenly reappear; and jelly-fish and starfish would be thrown up on the sand, along with planks, dead sea-birds, and green glass balls from fishermen's nets. Most of the fishing was done by trawlers, which operated from Courtown and Arklow, sometimes pitching about alarmingly in the high waves. On Thursdays the trawlers were especially busy, because, as my mother explained, Friday was a fast day. 'But why is Friday faster than any other day?' 'No, no; not *that* kind of fast! If you fast, it means you don't have anything to eat. The RCs believe it's a good thing to fast on Fridays out of respect for God – or at least not to eat any meat. Fish is all right, though.' Knowing the taste of Wexford fish, I thought the arrangement was a pretty shrewd compromise. From time to time one heard complaints about the scarcity of fish; but there must have been some about because every few days a seal would poke his head above the surface, or the fin of a porpoise could be seen moving south in a series of curving dives.

Sometimes, just before dusk, the word would go round that the Rickerbys were going to do some shore-fishing. Then we would all

The Bungalow, Ballymoney, built by the author's uncle for £300 in 1929/30.

The author (left) with friend in the 1930s at Ballymoney beach on Courtown Bay north of Wexford.

troop down to the north beach, where the sand sloped more gradually and there were no submerged rocks. There, on the soft white
sand at the top of the beach, lay the *Lucky Girl*. About sixteen feet
long and stoutly made, she had once been a ship's lifeboat. Now
she was painted royal blue, with red lead on her bottom and a
white stripe around the gunwales. Though she could not point
into the wind, having no centre-board, she sailed well under her
coarse brown mainsail. But, for fishing, her mast was unstepped
and all the sailing gear removed. Wooden ways were laid across
the sand; a roller of about eight inches in diameter was laid across
them and set against the bow. Then, as we all lifted, someone
shoved the roller under the boat, and her descent to the sea began.
When she reached the surf, the net was loaded onto her floor-
boards. This net was about five feet deep, with corks along the top
and lead weights along the bottom; it smelt strongly of creosote.
When all was ready, two ropes from one end of the net were held
on shore, and the boat was pushed out. One man rowed her slowly
around in an arc, while another paid out the net. They landed
thirty or forty yards along the beach, and then both ends of the net
were slowly hauled in, while the two groups converged. Excitement grew as yard after yard of the wet brown meshes was pulled
ashore. Then the belly of the net became visible. What would be
in it this time? One final heave, and the whole lot came out of the
surf and lay on the hard damp sand. Sometimes there would be
nothing but a crab, a couple of dog-fish, and patches of green sea-
weed. The dog-fish would be thrown up the beach to die. 'Hey',
said a visitor, 'what are you doing that for?' 'The dog-fish is no use
to man or beast.' 'Well, maybe not, but you'd get a few bob if you
sold them in Moore Street!' If the fishermen were lucky, there
might be a couple of dozen flat-fish – dabs, plaice with their
orange spots, the narrower sole, and perhaps even a small diamond-shaped ray with its spine ending in a thin tail. The still flapping fish would be thrown into baskets, and then people would
make for home. Back in the Bungalow the big ornate lamp would
already be lit, casting its glow around the table. After supper I
would take my candle and climb into the top bunk at the seaward
end of the building. Before dropping off I would hear, from out in
the quiet darkness, the rhythmic hiss of the surf.

In those early years a lot of work had to be done. Cartloads of gravel were dumped inside the gate, and we would carry it up in buckets and spread it in front of the bungalow. Any large stone that was at all striking in colour would be manhandled up from the beach and laid down to form a rockery. Trees already gave some privacy from the road below; but now fuchsia was planted for colour, and the slope down to the river was covered with Rose of Sharon. A bird table was erected, and the robins, chaffinches and yellowhammers gave pleasure to Grandpa as he sat in his chair. (But the platform had to project well beyond the post in order to defeat the occasional rat which came up from the river.) Up behind the house, gorse and scrub were burnt and uprooted to make space for vegetables and fruit. Not that our efforts were always successful. The apple trees did not do particularly well, and it was amazing how many birds could get under the nets to raid the strawberries. On a patch of ground to the west, Jimmy Mac-Donald built a one-room hut in about 1934 to take the place of the bell tent which had stood there before. When bunks were installed it meant that nine people at least could be fitted in on the site as a whole. When day visitors arrived, a dozen or more had to be fed from that tiny sweltering kitchen. The cooking and house-keeping were done by Aunt Connie and my mother, with occasional help from Molly Egan and others. In all that time they never had what could be called a proper holiday. This seemed to be accepted quite happily by all. If, in later years, anyone mentioned the fact, they would say that they loved the family, or that they enjoyed giving pleasure to others – comments which, however true, did nothing to remove one's feelings of guilt.

On wet days, when the grey clouds rolled up from the south west and the rain drummed on the roof, we read Dorothy L. Sayers, or Agatha Christie, or 'Sapper', or Dornford Yates. I was vaguely aware that the first two gave a very stylized picture of English society, and that the stories about Bulldog Drummond and the exquisite Berry were riddled with chauvinism and snobbery. But who cared? It was exciting stuff, and that was what most light popular fiction was like. Even the benign Wodehouse and the cynical Waugh (who were too advanced for us anyway) celebrated the very features that they mocked. A schoolboys' detective, like Sexton Blake, was just a sort of juvenile Sapper. Thus at some point R.S.V. Purvale could be relied on to give our foreign friend a jolly good uppercut. Apart from books, there was an excellent game called Bob, which was a primitive form of snooker played on a shiny wooden surface with pockets at each corner. Instead of balls there were chunky wooden rings about an inch in diameter, one set red and one green, which you potted by using a black ring as a cue-ball. At other times we would move the 'forms' up to the table and play cards. (The 'forms' were wooden benches; it was years before I realized that the forms at school originated in that way.) The most popular card games were Happy Families, Noah (a variation of the same idea, in which one collected father, mother and baby of a species and put them into the ark), Lexicon, and Old Maid (who was represented as an elderly owl reading Ovid in bed). Monopoly did not reach Ballymoney until the beginning of the war. My Uncle Ernest, who was a doctor in London and spent a fortnight in Ballymoney every year, condemned the game. 'It appeals to people's greed, and encourages them to gamble on the stock exchange.' I understood nothing about the stock exchange, but I resented the first bit, perhaps because I knew it was true. *My* only reservation about Monopoly was that it took too long. Riches or ruin did not come quickly enough.

There was no wireless in Ballymoney, but someone had bought a portable gramophone. As we were a rather low-brow lot, the top of our range was a selection from Gilbert and Sullivan. Below that there were songs by Jack Buchanan ('Leave a little for me'), Bob and Alf Pearson ('Little Dutch Mill'), Rudy Vallee ('If I had a girl like you'), and Layton and Johnson ('The clouds will soon roll by'). Irish songs included 'Little Nellie Cassidy' and 'The Old Bog Road'. The last verse of the former went:

> Little Nellie Cassidy earns fourteen pounds or more
> In waiting on the quality or answering the door.
> But her heart is some place far away upon the Wexford shore.
> Her heart is some place far away up-on the Wexford shore.

We liked that, because we thought she must have come from somewhere near Ballymoney. The Old Bog Road was a mournful dirge about an Irish exile in New York who thinks about his dead mother. We always sang it in a spirit of parody, with an exaggerated 'Oirish' accent: 'And there was I on Broadway with building breeks my lawd,/When they carried out her co-o-ffin to the awld bog rawd'. Intentional comedy was provided by the Western brothers (two pseudo-toffs and a piano). The last verse of 'The Old School Tie', which I only half understood, ran 'Gandhi's disciples all kicked up a din,/For Gandhi said "If we fight, we can win";/Then his loincloth fell off, but he wasn't run in;/He was wearing his owld schole tay.' There was also Jimmy O'Dea's dialogue with Harry O'Donovan called 'The Next Train'. Harry O'Donovan is an exasperated American who has come to a small country station expecting to pick up a train which will take him to Dublin on the first leg of a whirlwind tour of England, France, and Belgium. He has reckoned without the Irish railways. A series of requests is frustrated by Jimmy O'Dea who, it turns out, is both porter and booking-clerk. Then a train is heard approaching. It puffs slowly through the station as O'Dea searches for his signalman's cap. By now the visitor can take no more. 'I've had enough of you and your one-horse railway. Is there a local director of the line living near? I wanna make a complaint.' 'Director? Yessir. Wait till I get me silk hat.' 'Your silk *hat*?' 'Yessir. *I'm* the director!'

About the time when they built the bungalow Uncle Stan and Aunt Connie acquired the coast guard station. Mr and Mrs Rickerby were to live all year round in no. 1, and the four other houses were to be rented out in the summer months to visitors and their families. Mrs Rickerby was a wiry no-nonsense Londoner who wore a pinafore and kept her hair in a bun. As well as taking a few PG's in the summer she kept a couple of dozen hens (white wyandottes and Rhode Island reds) in a run behind the wall, letting them out every day to wander over a grassy bank at the bottom of the road. Mr Rickerby, considerably older, was a retired seaman who had started his career in the big sailing ships. Now he took life easy, growing vegetables and smoking his pipe. This indolence sometimes provoked his wife; but Old Rick, who had weathered many a storm in the south Atlantic, used to say 'When she blows up, I lets her blow on until she blows out'. Except when one of their sons was on leave from the navy, their only companion was Skipper, a powerful mongrel, who regarded the place as his and savaged any dog which smelt as if it thought otherwise.

On taking over the station, Uncle Stan had lavatories installed in the outhouses that ran along the back. These took the place of a small brick structure in the top corner of the grounds twenty yards from the main building. This structure, which was approached through the rose-gardens and was named accordingly, consisted of two very cramped compartments, each containing a plank with a hole in the middle. The coast guard service, it seems, did not mollycoddle its personnel.

As you faced the station, the land sloping down to the road was divided into roughly two-thirds and one-third by a steep pebbly drive. The third on the right remained as meadow, the far left was cultivated in a desultory way by Old Rick; the centre was now reshaped into three tiers – tennis court, croquet lawn, and general playground. The tennis court sloped slightly towards the north-east corner, and if you skied a volley in that direction the ball would fly over the wire and end up in Mr Rickerby's potatoes; and as you tramped up and down the drills trying to find it you might be barked at by the old sea-dog himself. Still, it was quite a good court, and it saw a lot of use. One opponent I enjoyed playing was Capt. Sugrue of the Irish army, a tall straight man with his greyish hair brushed straight back and a neatly clipped moustache. 'Come on Rudd,' he would say in a stern voice, 'I'll beat you this time'. But his technique was against him, for he held the racquet vertically with the head uppermost, and instead of swinging his arm he would thrust it forward like a boxer. As the bounces were not very high, he had to spend much of the time with his knees bent, in the manner of Groucho Marx, and a really low ball was always a winner. Another visitor, a little older than myself, was Joe Hackett. Even then, there was nothing wrong with *his* technique. Noticing his talent, his parents wisely had him coached, and ten years later he was the best player in the country.

On the croquet lawn we played a variation called golf croquet. As soon as a player got through a hoop, everyone went on to the next; and though you could hit an opponent's ball out of position, there were no roquets. All this made for a faster game. One day when I was playing by myself, aged nine or ten, I realized that a pair of grown-ups was sitting watching me. So I asked if they'd like to play. The lady smiled in a rather peculiar way, but the gentleman, a Mr Corbally, said 'Why not?' and got to his feet. This process took some time, for he was well over six foot. He was also unusually thin and seemed to be built in sections, so that he swayed in and out in unexpected places. (In retrospect I am reminded of the diplomat Lord Erne and his rather stout vivacious wife. At a reception someone said 'Ah, here come storeyed Erne and animated bust'.) Anyhow – the first clear hint that something was amiss came when Mr Corbally weighed the mallet in his right hand. 'Is that what you're used to, darling?' asked his wife, still smiling. 'Not quite. This one's about three pounds.' By the second round it was clear that Mr Corbally had got used to the mallet and to the slant of the lawn; he was bringing off some shots which he had simply no right to get. Afterwards, down at the Bungalow, I observed in some annoyance 'Old Corbally's surprisingly good at croquet.' 'I should think he is,' said Uncle Stan. 'He's the Irish champion.'

Another grown-up who strode into my consciousness was Uncle Herbert (Uncle Stan's older brother). There was something larger than life about Uncle Herbert. A tall impressive-looking man with a fine baritone voice, which he had used in amateur theatricals, he would often come to the Bungalow on a fine morning before anyone was up, clad in a huge multi-coloured towel. 'Awake!' he boomed, 'for morning in the bowl of night/Has flung the stone that puts the stars to flight;/And lo, the hunter of the east has caught/The sultan's turret in a noose of light.' He would then announce that he had had his morning dip, and that the water was just like a hot bath. Eventually, having done his damage, he would retreat to the sound of groans and imprecations. Some grown-ups were known to us only by rude or malicious nicknames. One small round man with shorts and thin legs was 'the egg on needles'; a lady in slacks, which were at that time rather suspect, was called 'the horse'; and then there was the apparently irredeemable pair 'the horrible woman and the horrible child'.

Mostly we played with other children – at rounders, or touch-and-pass, or 'larky' (a form of hide and seek). We also flew kites, climbed rocks, fished for crabs with limpets on a bent pin, gathered blackberries, and slid down a steep grass cliff on a surfboard, ending up in a pile of soft sand. And then there was Tara Hill. I made one early expedition with a boy called Robert Mills from Lancashire. When we first met, I said 'You sound funny.' 'So do you,' he answered. After that we hit it off well and decided to climb Tara Hill. We bought some bottles of fizzy lemonade and two large bags of liquorice allsorts, and started on our way. As it was hot on the way up I took off my new grey and pink pullover and tied it round my waist by the sleeves. An hour later we reached the top and surveyed the county from a cairn of stones. Soon afterwards, by now rather weary, we set off on the way down. As we approached Ballymoney, I suddenly realized that my pullover was gone and also that I was beginning to feel extremely sick. I spent the next two days in bed with a violent bilious attack, and have never eaten a liquorice allsort since. Amongst the children in that same year was a pair of sisters, Geraldine and Petra, also from England. One day, with the aid of some bath towels, they put on a strip tease. Goodness knows where they got the idea, but the boys had sense enough not to run away. At the time I knew it was interesting, but *why* was a mystery. A voice also whispered it was wrong to find it interesting; but *why* it was wrong was another mystery. Since no inducements had been offered in the form of lollipops or bulls' eyes, the girls' motive must have been simply to put on a display before an appreciative audience. And I suppose that in adult life, when money and sex have been taken into account, strip tease still remains a part of show business.

After the Bungalow, one of the first houses to be built was Whitewalls, which belonged to Dr W.A. Cooke (Uncle Willie). Standing on the same side of the valley, but further inland and further back from the river and the road, this was a substantial two-storey modern house with a flat roof and wide casement windows in metal frames. Across the front ran a large lounge, divided by a French window, which opened onto a pinkish concrete terrace. Whether from loyalty or indifference, no one said anything at the time. But it has to be admitted that, in the setting of Ballymoney, Whitewalls was an embarrassing lapse of taste. Luckily there was a line of trees along the riverbank which hid it from passers-by. As Whitewalls went up, water had to be located, and I watched in amazement as the water-diviner walked slowly up and down, holding a hazel twig lightly in his hands. Eventually the twig began to jerk, and a well was sunk on the rising ground behind the house. Perhaps in the next hundred years someone will explain how water-divining works, or else prove it false. In the meantime it remains a slightly eerie element in common experience, like the infectiousness of yawning.

Uncle Willie, a cousin of my mother's, had a practice near Phoenix Park on the North Circular Road. He was also the prison doctor in Mountjoy jail. Mercifully there were few murders during those years; but when someone was hanged Uncle Willie had the gruesome task of inspecting the corpse and issuing the certificate. For days before and after the execution he was in a state of depression, pondering whether to resign from the post. In normal circumstances he got on well with the inmates, for he was a cheerful and kindly man; so it was easy to imagine him being urged to continue in a job which few would have coveted. But in the end, after several years, he did get out. His wife (Aunt Kathleen) was a brisk, efficient woman. She had strongly conservative opinions, of the West Briton kind, for which she argued with great energy and assurance. 'Really, what *does* de Valera think he's doing? He's going to put this country back in the middle ages. As long as this nonsense goes on, the North will *never* come in. And quite right too!' This combative quality distinguished her from my other aunts, who in general disliked arguments and avoided them as a threat to domestic peace. Aunt Kathleen also set her social sights a bit higher than we did. She dressed in a smart and fairly expensive style, and retained a trim figure well into her sixties. This was recognized by the other women with just a hint of Christian acerbity. 'Yes, Kathleen does her exercises every day.' 'Good for her, of course.' 'Hmmm, nice to have the time.' In the early 30s her maiden name became von Hoffe, instead of merely Hoffe. But after 1939 the von was quietly dropped, and it was discovered that her people were actually South African rather than German. This social confidence did not mean that she lived a separate existence from the rest of us. During the summer months, assisted by the tireless and indestructible Mary Pigeon from Tara Hill, she ran Whitewalls as a guest-house for her own circle of acquaintances.

But it was a guest-house where there were cocktails in the lounge and where she presided at dinner in a long dress. How this could be done for three guineas a week, even at 1935 prices, I do not know; but it was. Aptly enough, she was known in the connection as 'The Countess' – no doubt with a glance at Yeats's Countess Cathleen.

Although I could see it would be a mistake to cross her, someone of my age had no reason to be afraid. In fact I liked her, partly because her ideas were clearly expressed and were seen to be, as it were, firm round the edges. She also made very good fudge. For grown-ups, relations with Aunt Kathleen were more tricky, especially if they belonged to that section of the local community which resented her and all that she stood for. In these years the disagreement came to focus on whether she and Uncle Willie had the legal right to make a short-cut to the beach by throwing a small footbridge across the river onto a piece of public land. On at least two occasions a bridge was built, and, almost before the concrete had set, it was broken up at night with crowbars and levered into the river. After much indignation and palaver a truce was arranged on condition that the bridge was limited to two highly impermanent-looking planks.

Another cause of vexation was that, as Jimmy MacDonald was finishing Whitewalls, Jimmy Clince was finishing his céilidh-hall a short way down river, between the far bank and the road. It was a smallish concrete building with windows that provided little ventilation. But when the noise and temperature became unbearable, a whole section of the tin roof could be pushed up on a hinge and propped open with a piece of timber. The only snag was that, when they literally raised the roof, they did so on the Whitewalls side of the dance-hall; the screen of trees did little to absorb the din. Yet if this was a nuisance to Aunt Kathleen and her guests, no doubt Jimmy Clince took a different view. Three nights a week his hall provided a much-needed centre where the people of the district could meet and socialize. As no liquor was allowed, there was no fighting or rowdiness or even bad language. Why should he be prevented from earning a few pounds by the sort of people who had had their own way in the country for far too long? Anyhow, the noise couldn't be as bad as all that; otherwise he would surely have had a solicitor's letter. As children, Tony Polden (Herbert's son), Joan, and I held a half-way position. Though we knew we didn't quite belong there, we found the céilidh-hall interesting; and Jimmy Clince, who stood at the entrance taking money, would let us nip in and sit on the bench near the door in our shorts and sweaters and bare feet. On a platform to the right was a three-piece band with fiddle, accordion and drums. Irish dances, which alternated with waltzes, were organized and set in motion by the rubicund Lar Kavanagh, a jolly round man in a black suit with neat feet and polished shoes. ('Two colleens here now please for the Walls of Limerick', 'One gent more now for the Siege of Ennis'.) Then Mr Kavanagh would join the dance himself, inserting all kinds of extra steps as his shoes twinkled. The whole scene was like that represented in William Trevor's 'Ballroom of Romance', but without any of the hopelessness and melancholy that make Trevor's such a haunting piece. As for 'The Siege of Ennis', I heard it for a long time as 'The Siege of Venice'. Picturing men with muskets standing in gondolas in the Lagoon, I wondered what that had to do with an Irish dance. Of course I could have asked, but you couldn't ask about *everything*; and there was always the risk of making an eejit of yourself.

Another structure that appeared in Ballymoney about this time in a field halfway up the road was a green single-decker bus. With curtains over the windows and a stove-pipe at the back, it looked more solid and comfortable than many a caravan. The owner was a Mr Jack Flood from Dublin, who bore some resemblance to the American film star Wallace Beery. Perhaps understandably, he was a little disconcerted when Joan asked him whether his family also lived in a bus in Rathmines. Rathmines, incidentally, used to be thought of as one of Dublin's posher districts. When music-hall comedians referred to it, they put on a 'refained' accent, as in the riddle 'What's the definition of sex?' 'I give up.' 'It's what the Rathmaines people keep their cowl in.' Nowadays that joke would elicit only groans.

Finally, near the top of the hill, on the left as you walked up the road, Mr Arthur Talbot Brady, a bank manager from Carlow, built a low, wide, cream-coloured house looking down towards the sea, and called it Darogue (Two Oaks). His son Donal was only a little older than me, and we spent quite a lot of time together. The Brady family had a small dark-brown pony called Jessie, which had clearly been bought because of her placid nature. When urged, she would start to trot, and then you had to grip with your knees and rise up and down in the saddle to avoid being jolted to pieces. But Jessie did not seem to have a higher gear. I never saw her break into a canter, much less a gallop. This rather low-key experience may have prevented me from having fantasies about careering across the fields on a powerful steed with warning of some terrible danger, and arriving just in time at the Gorey Garda station. But Donal and I certainly had fantasies about small boats. We had seen a couple of dinghies in Courtown harbour, and we would describe in detail, as we lay on a headland chewing grass, how we would scrape them, paint them, rig them, and then sail them to Dublin.

One summer, just after I had arrived, Donal said, 'Do you know what?' 'What?' 'I've built a boat.' 'Go 'way.' 'Honest. We'll launch her this afternoon, but you'll have to come up and give us a hand. Big Jack Leary's going to lend us his handcart.' The boat turned out to be just over four feet long and shaped, ominously, like a young person's coffin. When this was pointed out, Donal agreed that it should be named *The Coffin*. The structure consisted of two sheets of plywood nailed vertically to a wooden floor and braced by a wooden stern and a couple of cross-pieces. The whole was liberally daubed with pitch, which did nothing to relieve the funereal effect. *The Coffin* proved surprisingly heavy, and it needed all Big Jack's muscle-power to load it onto the handcart. Moreover, as Donal had noticed that the height was greater than the width and that there was likely to be a problem of stability, he had procured a section of iron girder, about three feet long, which was to be laid on the bottom as ballast before launching. The girder too went into the handcart. And finally the paddle was thrown in on top. That was a brush-handle, nailed to something that looked as if it had once been a cupboard door. On the far shore conditions were perfect. The receding tide had left a shallow lagoon about three feet deep. So when Donal seated himself rather painfully on the girder I pushed him off. *The Coffin* immediately keeled over to the right, and I had to wade in and grab it from behind. After a while, by keeping his body motionless and paddling with the gentlest of strokes, Donal inched almost imperceptibly forward. But any more energetic movement at once threw him sideways. An hour later the project had been ruefully abandoned. *The Coffin* was hauled up the beach, and a week later, when it had dried out, it made quite a merry blaze. No doubt the Vikings, who used to visit Wexford, would have approved.

Donal was a good talker. Sometimes what he had to say was didactic, e.g. how to lessen the impact of a Christian Brother's leather on a schoolboy's hand. Sometimes it was sheer entertainment, like his imitation of the good Mrs Peters in the Railway Hotel in Gorey: 'Hello Doh-doh; come into the bar now and have an orange car-oosh!' But on one miserable occasion all his high spirits were quenched. His father had had a stroke and died. That evening, Aunt Kathleen arranged for Donal, with his younger brother and sister, to come down to Whitewalls; Joan and I were brought over from the Bungalow to lend support. But it was no good. The three children just sat on the sofa and wept; no words brought any comfort. It was the first time that I associated Ballymoney with death. *Et in Arcadia ego.*

From 1936 onwards even the young were dimly aware that ugly things were happening in the world. We had heard snatches of talk about General O'Duffy and his Blueshirts in Spain. We had sung, to the tune of 'Roll along, covered waggon, roll along', the verse beginning 'Will you come to Abyssinia, will you come?/ Bring your own ammunition and your gun.' Threatening noises were now coming from Germany. There was even 'a courtesy visit' from the battleship *Schleswig-Holstein*. It attracted a lot of attention as it lay at the quayside in Dublin, with its high meccano-like tower; and it led to a new spate of (slightly uneasy?) jokes about the Irish navy, which consisted of two fishery protection vessels called *The Fort Rannoch* and *The Muirchu*. Still, life in Dublin, as in Ballymoney, jogged along pleasantly enough. As you drove out to Clontarf, you passed the familiar pubs and pawnshops of the North Strand; you saw placards saying 'Andrews Liver Salts – I must have left it behind', 'Guinness is good for you', and 'Ah, Bisto!' Overhead a small aeroplane might be writing 'Persil' in white smoke against a blue sky. Children played impartially with the old (like chestnuts, which, when seasoned in the airing cupboard, made excellent 'conkers') and the new (like the yo-yo, which was demonstrated by a young American virtuoso in Clery's). On the radio, in 'Monday night at eight' Inspector Hornley investigated ('You see he gave himself away'), and Sid Walker asked 'Any rags, bottles or bones?' 'Band Waggon', with Big-hearted Arthur Askey and Stinker Murdoch, was just beginning. In music, echoes were still received from the wild west ('Old Faithful', 'Waggon Wheels'), and romance throve from 'South of the Border' to 'The Isle of Capree'. The last two were great favourites with Maggie Gannon. She also liked the rather bogus Irish nostalgia that was beamed across the Atlantic ('Does your mother come from Ireland?', 'When Irish eyes are smiling'). The home-grown variety came from Athlone, as John McCormack sang 'Macushla', 'Mother Macree' and 'I met her in the garden where the praties grow' – a tradition that, one sensed, was now becoming rather thin. In England George V had died; Edward VIII had come, and then retired with his Duchess to a diplomatic limbo; George VI had been crowned. At home Dev was firmly in control, with his bifocal vision of a Gaelic Catholic Ireland embracing the six counties. Sinister personalities came before us in papers, radio bulletins and newsreels. But if you missed them it didn't really matter, because the really interesting people were all on cigarette cards. By a long process of exchange and cajolery I had acquired a set of cricketers, English and Australian. These could be supplemented by borrowing Joan's film stars. The racehorses, like Barham and Windsor Lad looked even more magnificent. But best of all were the cars – saloons, sports cars, and racing machines like the green ERA, the white Mercedes, and the red Maserati.

In 1938 my grandfather died; Maggie left; and we moved to a small house in Castle Avenue. It was hoped that this new situation would bring my parents closer together. But this proved to be an illusion. So in the spring of the following year my mother asked if I would like to go to the Methodist College in Belfast as a boarder. The link here was the Rev. Alec MacRae, who was on the board of governors and also Principal of Edgehill, the Methodist training college. Years before, when he was a student, 'Uncle Alec' had fallen ill and had been taken in and looked after by my grandparents. He had remained on close terms with the family ever since. It was now proposed that, if I did adequately in a set of exam papers, I might be given a residence scholarship in the school. I sat the papers in High School and news eventually came that I had passed. (No one ever mentioned whether there were any competitors.) It was a strange time to leave Dublin, but the atmosphere at home was now so unpleasant that even the prospect of a boarding school seemed attractive. So, as war loomed, I put away my lead soldiers, packed my cases, and took the train to Belfast with my mother. In Edgehill College on Sunday 3 September at 12.15pm the wireless was switched on, and Neville Chamberlain's thin, sad voice came on the air: 'I have to tell you that no such undertaking has been received, and that consequently this country is at war with Germany.' On the following morning, with mingled curiosity and apprehension, I entered Bedell, the junior boarding-house at the Methodist College.

Belfast

Methodist College, or 'Methody', was (and is) a Victorian Gothic building of red brick, built on a strip of rising land between Malone Road and Lisburn Road about a mile south of the city centre. MacArthur Hall, the girls' boarding-house, was on the same site, at the Lisburn Road end. Across the front ran College Gardens, a private road with a terrace of tall, solidly prosperous houses, many of them occupied by doctors or dentists. The whole area was surrounded by splendid iron railings, which, if one includes the concrete base, stood some eight feet high. Within a short time all the railings had been brutally amputated and carted away, leaving a row of pathetic stumps. The same mindless vandalism was repeated times without number throughout the United Kingdom. No one seems to know where the railings went; but there is a persistent rumour that not one of them was used for the war effort.

On your left as you went up the drive was a collection of huts, put there on a purely temporary basis in the first world war. They were large but draughty, and in one of them the wind, as it came down the stove-pipe, intermittently produced the opening notes of Beethoven's Violin Concerto. Every time this happened, James McAteer, a maths teacher, was forced to complete the phrase in his head. In the end, fearing for his sanity, he moved to another room, his place being taken by a less musical colleague. Before the front entrance the lawn was now torn up to provide a large tank of water in case of fire. This, though sad, was defensible. (Similarly 'Inst.', an elegant eighteenth-century school building near the city centre, had to turn over its front lawn to a barrage balloon.) What no one seemed able to justify was wrecking the rugby field by throwing up a series of earthworks, supposedly to give protection against blast and flying shrapnel. Yet it was hard to imagine a game taking place in the middle of an air raid; and in its ruined state the pitch could be used for no purpose at all. In the main building the basement and some ground-floor windows disappeared behind sandbags, and all the other windows were covered with black paint. For the next six years daylight could only be obtained by admitting large quantities of very fresh air.

During class hours everyone had to carry a gas mask. In those first weeks of the phoney war, gas mask drill gave scope for horseplay. The sight of a not-greatly loved face disappearing behind a layer of perspex and black rubber was always irresistible; the more so as the master could only shout a reprimand by removing the apparatus and thus exposing himself to supposedly deadly fumes. In class most people would put their gas mask boxes on the floor. One more fastidious chap, however, who sat in front of me, had a special sort of coloured cylinder which he wore all the time, slung over his shoulder with a piece of white cord. For some reason I found this irritating; so one day I took a very sharp pen-knife, crawled up behind him as he sat at his desk, and delivered one short slash. The tin crashed to the floor with a satisfying clatter. Unfortunately the stroke laid open a two-inch gash across my classmate's jacket. The knife was confiscated by 'Johnny the Hawk' (Mr John Falconer, Vice-Principal) and was never seen again; and in due course I received a large bill from an invisible mender which proved difficult to justify to my mother. No doubt I was lucky to get off with that. At night there was ARP (air raid precautions) drill. '1. Close all windows before putting on the light. 2. Put on your dressing-gown. 3. Take your gas mask and sleeping bag and walk in an orderly way to the nearest staircase. 4. Report to the master on duty in the basement.' It was hard to believe that all this fuss had any serious purpose. Yet somewhere, terrible things were happening. There had been a photo in the paper of the *Schleswig-Holstein*, last seen in Dublin, pulverizing the port of Danzig.

Early in 1941 the aircraft carrier HMS *Biter* put into Belfast, and one of its officers, Leonard I'Anson, who was a family friend, took me out for the afternoon to show me over his ship. This proved an interesting but quite a strenuous exercise. Years later I learned that his shipmates had been astonished at the amount of good white bread, specially baked for the wardroom, that could be packed into the stomach of a small thirteen-year-old boy. School fare was drab in the extreme. Spam and dried egg were among the more attractive items. Once a week dessert consisted of a plate of tepid ground rice, like decorators' paste, with a blob of carrot jam in the middle. No doubt Hitler was as much to blame for this as our catering officer; but hers was the more visible presence. Miss MacMillan was a tall lady with striking features. Though not unkindly, she had the misfortune to resemble an engraving of King Lear in the Thunderstorm which Eric Fraser had done for the *Radio Times*. She was therefore called Lear – an appropriate name, perhaps, for one who presided over so many culinary disasters. Various techniques evolved for distracting attention from the food. As we stood behind our chairs waiting for a house master to say the Latin grace, a boy would be addressed by the neighbour on his right. When he turned round again he would find that the jacket potato on his side plate had been mashed by the heel of someone's hand. Or again, when seated, you could place your right shin behind your neighbour's left calf and then bring your left leg across the front. As the pressure increased, those sitting nearby would notice a boy silently disappearing under the table, his face contorted in agony. You, meanwhile, would be engaged in conversation with the person on your left. This kind of behaviour was rationalized as a form of protest, not wholly without justification. Our plight may be gauged from the fact that after lunch on Tuesdays and Thursdays, when we wore our Army Cadet Force uniform, a concerted rush was made across Malone Road to the NAAFI canteen, where huge wedges of pie and great slabs of cake were swilled down with mugfuls of sweet tea.

School food was one strand in a rope of misery which, paradoxically, bound the new intake together. Another was one of those initiation rituals which seem to occur in so many male institutions and are designed to convince the youngest and weakest of their inferiority. In the first week after our arrival we were told to report, one by one, to the top dorm, where the senior, fourteen-year olds slept. As he came in, each boy had to run down the centre of the dorm naked to the waist, while he was beaten from each side with knotted towels. That was called 'running the gauntlet'. Then his head was ducked in a basin of cold water. And finally he had to bend over a bed while his backside was beaten with a gym-shoe – one blow from each member of the dorm. This ordeal, which was called 'a skiting', might be repeated at any sign of disrespect to the dominant group. In 1941 MacArthur Hall was taken over as government offices and the girl boarders were transferred to one end of the main building. This meant that we saw them every day at meals as well as in class. I don't know if their presence had anything to do with the decline of the macho initiation-rites, but at any rate we abandoned the practice in Bedell, and did not have to face such treatment on entering the senior houses.

Towards the end of the first year a web of common interest began to develop which made school life bearable. But the first two terms were very bleak. As an outsider I was especially vulnerable. One or two boys who particularly disliked me would call me an IRA man, which would have surprised my West Briton relatives. My speech must have sounded strange, and I for my part had to get used to the accent and idiom of the Ulster Scots. 'Hey, Wullay. D'ye maind that fawx tarrier?' 'Aye, I maind him well.' 'Alec MacLintock wanted to buy him.' 'Catch yourself on,' I said. 'Why, are ye not sallin?' 'Ye know raightly I'm not sallin,' I said. 'What about ould Jawhn that you got him from?' said Alec, 'has he anny more?' 'I doubt he's no more,' I said. 'And annyway he's a carnaptious and bloodymainded ould sawd.' 'He is surely,' said Alec. 'When I bought him,' I said, 'it took me a brave long taime. You'd think I was askin' for somethin' like a praize bule instead of a wee dawg.' Along with this speech went shared allusions to well-loved places like Cookstown, Fintana, Fivemiletown, and Dungannon. And in those early days a homesick boy could sometimes be heard singing softly in his cubicle, 'It is old but it is beauteeful, its colours they are fine./'Twas worn at Derry, Aughrim, Enniskillen, and the Boyne./My father wore it long ago in byegone days of yore./So it's on the twelfth I love to wear the sash my father wore'. Later on, renderings of 'The Sash' and other tribal lays like 'The Ould Orange Flute' and 'We Fight For No Surrender' became noticeably less frequent. I wonder why. Was it because the boys were growing up and becoming educated? Or was it because the war had now started in earnest, and sectarian issues were being shelved? Or was it because the people's minds were fully occupied with school affairs? In any case, one thing that I began to suspect then, and am now certain of, is that Northern Ireland's troubles have very little to do with theological disagreements.

In our second year the Medical Officer, Dr James Smylie, had one bad idea which fortunately didn't last long. It was that before bedtime Nurse Quinton should come round and administer regular doses of cod liver oil. Each boy had to stand outside his cubicle and have a spoonful of the nauseating liquid put into his mouth. He then had to say 'Thank you, nurse'; so there was no hope of stealing away to the hand basins. Another hazard was a master who, after putting out the lights, would stand outside the door and listen for an outbreak of talk. Then he would burst in and deal out punishment. Once, after he had said good-night and withdrawn, a courageous soul shouted, 'Hey, Crawly! Are ye lestnin' at the dure?' This of course made it impossible for the man to re-enter without acknowledging both his name and his treachery. On another occasion, just before lights-out, we smelt a pungent odour coming from one of the cubicles. Someone was attempting to smoke a stick of cinnamon. At the same time the master-on-duty's footsteps were heard approaching. That night it was supposed to be Dr Ranson, of whom we were rather scared. So there were a few seconds of feverish activity. 'Hey! Put out that fag!' 'Open the windy.' 'Ye *can't* open the windy; there's a bloody blackout!' 'Well, shake your dressin'-gown or somethin'.' Then, to everyone's surprise, in walked the mysterious Dr Rudnidsky. He was a dark, romantic-looking man; and since no one knew much about him he was the focus of odd rumours. Thus, as well as being a mathematician (which he *was*), he was also supposed to be a brilliant sprinter, a virtuoso violinist, and a high-ranking officer in Polish intelligence. I seized a tin of rather smelly dubbin and a rag, and held them in front of his face. 'Just doing my ruggerboots, sir!' He drew heavily on a black cigarette, blew out a cloud of perfumed smoke, and said, 'Goodnight, gentlemen.'

Towards the end of term the spirit of anarchy was hard to suppress. Like High School, Methody too had a sergeant, but of a larger, slower and more taciturn breed. The nickname 'Blarge', though never wholly explained, seemed to suit him. One night a boy in pyjamas ran past his room, which was not far from our dormitory, and with a shout of 'Bully old Blarge!' vanished round the corner. He was followed by someone who burst a balloon, then by someone who produced the beginning of the last post on a bugle, and finally by a boy who hurled a large empty tin against his door. That did it. As the boy disappeared, the door opened and Blarge stepped into the corridor. He was wearing the navy-blue trousers of his uniform with braces over a long-sleeve vest. As he adjusted his tin glasses he roared 'If I catch any of you young ruffians I'll make you sting for it!' The next evening a boy of unimpeachable Methodist connections (now a professor of physiology) managed to set off a large fire extinguisher, covering much of the upper landing with foam. This brought solemn words from the house master; next time the cane would *certainly* be used.

The Principal at that time was J.W. Henderson, a large beefy man with a blustering manner. We rarely saw him except at morning assembly, where he wore a well-cut suit of light grey, with patent leather shoes and a lavender cravat. Occasionally he would introduce some distinguished speaker to the whole school. One such speaker was Sir Ronald Storrs – scholar, diplomat, and friend of Lawrence of Arabia. At the end of his introduction the Head said

... and Sir Ronald has recorded it all in his admirable volume entitled *Orientations*. His manifold experiences are well summarized in what Browning once called a chorus-ending of Euripides – a chorus-ending quoted as a conclusion by Sir Ronald himself. I shall now give you the original Greek, boys and girls. Pollai morphai ton daimonion. Polla ... How does it go, Sir Ronald?

Storrs, obligingly, 'polla d'aelptos krainousi theoi.' 'Yes yes indeed; polla d'aelptos ... ahem. Here, anyhow, is a literal translation ... There are many forms of divinity. The gods bring many things to pass ... isn't that it, Sir Ronald?' Storrs, slightly wearily, 'The gods bring many things to pass *unexpectedly*.' 'Quite so; *unexpectedly*. Well, I shan't translate the next bit, boys and girls; but the *gist* of it is that often we don't accomplish what we expect to do.'

Every morning, after the Head had announced the hymn, Dr Ernest Stoneley would rise from his chair, walk thinly and jerkily to the front of the platform, and check with a swift sweep of his left hand that his waistcoat and fly were safely buttoned. Then he would raise his right hand and conduct both the orchestra (Miss Sarah Garvin, organ, plus sundry strings) and the assembled school. Stoneley was a first-rate violinist – leader, in fact, of the Philharmonic Orchestra. The navy, it was said, had used his phenomenal hearing to listen for submarine engines in the first world war. More doubtful was the tale that after being torpedoed he had swum twenty miles to the coast of Japan. This seemed even harder to believe when he appeared at the swimming pool in Pirrie Park with his bony frame clad in an Edwardian bathing costume. Musicians have always puzzled me. One assumes they have a more sensitive ear than anybody else. Yet I have never heard a foreign conductor speak with a recognizably English accent. Doubtless ours are just as bad in German or Italian. So too when Dr Stoneley began to speak, a cracked Lancashire voice issued from his crooked benevolent face. Useless, I suppose, to try to regularize genius.

I saw more of his colleague, the plump and sweet-natured Miss Garvin. This was because the Latin master, finding that I had done a year of the language already, told me to go away and come back next session. So I was sent to Miss Garvin for piano lessons. I did a couple more examinations with something called The Associated Board; and once, with two friends, I had to compete in a piano competition down town, adjudicated by Mr Maurice Jacobson. All three of us got prizes (presumably everyone else did too); so we were taken to tea by Miss Garvin in a café in Lombard Street, where we ordered sausages and eggs. One of the pieces I learned for her was Mendelssohn's 'Spring Song'. Sadly, that marked the height of my attainment, for other interests were pushing music out. Moreover, I had begun to work out chord sequences (initially just in C and F) for the dance-tunes of the thirties and early forties. So as 'Spring Song' and Brahms's 'Lullaby' began to recede, 'Stardust' and 'Moonlight Serenade' took their place. A poor exchange, to be sure, but one which grew into an agreeable pastime.

The school made its pupils sample a range of subjects between the ages of twelve and fourteen. 'Who takes you for drawing?'

asked my house master, the gentle and civilized George Wareham. I was eager to tell him, but didn't know the name. So I blurted out excitedly, 'Oh he's a huge fat man with a bald head, and glasses like the bottoms of lemonade bottles!' Wareham nodded quietly, and with his pipe clenched tightly between his teeth said, 'Yes Rudd, I *think* I know who you mean.' For engineering we went to 'the shop', an impressive place with work-benches around the walls, and a dozen or more machines in the centre, gleaming behind their wire cages. Overhead was an elaborate system of belts and wheels. Presumably if you were any good you progressed to lathes and grinders and things, but I never got that far. The first day, after telling us to put on our jackets (khaki-coloured blouses with perished elastic around the waist), Mr Ned Hinton named the implements which hung on a frame in front of each boy. 'These are yer tewls' (the vowel was narrowed like the French u). 'First, yer outside callipers; then, yer inside callipers. And this is yer ball-pean hammer' (I *think* I've got that right). Then he described some basic techniques. 'There are two types of solderin'. One is called tennin', and the other's called swattin'.' After a couple of weeks of this preparation we started to make metal paperweights. Mine was about four inches high, in the form of a lighthouse with a breaking wave. After hacking the thing out of sheet metal, bending it, and riveting it to its base, I showed it to Mr Hinton. 'As a jawb, it's ... well, there's not much you can do with it; but you can take your file and polish it up.' So I did that, and then put it in a cupboard until next week, by which time it was a mass of discoloration and rust. So every week I filed away at the lighthouse, and at the end of term took home a wafer-thin object, which I conveniently lost.

Science wasn't much better. My friend Basil McIvor and I listened to Mr J.R. Brown, an ancient Scot, explaining the usual things. We conducted our experiments, recording how the lime-water turned milky and the litmus paper red or blue. It was during a disquisition on alkalies and acids that I said to McIvor, 'Ask him if that's the principle behind stomach-powders'. My friend put up his hand. Brown's head slowly pivoted on the reptilian neck. 'Eh ... eh. Is there a question heer?' McIvor asked the question. 'Eh ... eh. *Whot's* that?' At this point, on seeing the expression on

Brown's face, McIvor should have contrived to withdraw. Instead he tried again: 'Sir, I was wondering if that was the principle behind stomach-powders.' An innocent enough question, but the old fellow must have sensed an element of subversive insolence behind it, because he flung McIvor out. Four years later, however, my friend got his revenge, when the humiliation was far more grievous.

Not everyone found the arts subjects any more congenial. One day the English master, who believed we should not only write about what we did in the holidays but also learn the basic structure of the language, was trying to explain the accusative or objective case. Noticing that one of the class was mystified, he said, 'Look here, Porter. The accusative of he is him. What's the accusative of she?' 'Shim,' said Porter. Sometimes, goaded beyond endurance, the pedagogue would come storming down the room. This was the signal for the miscreant to cover up, by resting his elbows on the desk, bending his head forward and locking his fingers across the back of his neck. Given the lack of room between the desks and the fact that the teacher was hampered by his gown, no physical harm was ever done, and we felt no sense of grievance. The girls, however, resented having to write impositions. 'Oh come on, sir. Give me a smack with the ruler. Here's my hand!' But no master was ever so ungallant, or so foolish, as to comply.

At fourteen or so, if you were going to do languages, you had to decide whether to take Greek or German in addition to Latin and French. German, for obvious reasons, was not popular; and it was taught by a sweet but rather elderly lady with little in the way of proselytizing zeal. The senior Classics master, on the other hand, was something of a rogue. Mr William Bullick ('Bos' to generations of pupils) was now in his early fifties. He was quite a handsome man with a noble forehead which, through some rather unusual hinge in his cranium, he could move backwards and forwards – a gesture usually accompanied by a pronounced blink and an adjustment to his tie. In virtue of his position he was able to prescribe which Latin textbook should be used throughout the school. Not surprisingly, it turned out to be his own. But he must also have had some higher motives; for although he had then written no corresponding work on Greek he would break into his colleagues' classes as the time for the fateful decision approached. 'Excuse me Misster Eh ... (he never managed to articulate his subordinates' names) ... I would just like to inform the boys and girls that next month they will be presented with a unique opportunity.' Then followed a eulogy of ancient Greece, ending in a practical peroration '... and not only will Greek give you the golden key to European literature and thought, it will also secure you an entry to the Diplomatic Corps and the higher echelons of the Civil Service. So speak earnestly to your parents; I'm sure they will not wish to sstand in your way.' As this message went round, it created the impression that you *had* to have Greek to get into the Civil Service. A French teacher, who naturally sided with the moderns in the long-standing *querelle*, became so annoyed at this that he took to following Bos, five minutes later, assuring the pupils that his sister was in the Civil Service and she didn't even know the Greek alphabet.

Bos, however, was not defeated. A fortnight before the Greek/German decision was due he burst in again. 'Excuse me, Misster Eh ... I just wish to say that I have prepared six stencilled sheets on the Greek achievement, starting from the triumph of Dr Schliemann, who excavated Troy from under six layers or sstrata, and proceeding down to the tragically early demise of Alexander the Great. A test will be set in a week's time, and there will be a prize of at least a pound for anyone who gets all the answers right.' He then swept out of the room leaving us on our own (the master having wisely nipped out for a smoke). Bos's voice, with its emphatic sibilants, seemed to invite imitation. So I hazarded, 'I have excavated Alexxander from under sixx layers of sstencils.' In a flash Bos was back, having only feigned a withdrawal. 'I heard ssome nasty little voice hissing like a ssnake. I repeat, this is a serious matter. Let there be no more nonsense.' In the end the sheets turned out to be straightforward enough, and the old blighter had managed to collect some impressive remarks about Greece from people whom I had heard of, like Goethe and Shelley. So after a friend had corrected my pronunciation ('Not Demostheens, you fathead, Demostheneese') I took the test and relieved Bos of a pound. As my weekly allowance was a shilling, I was confused by this sudden affluence and wrote to my mother to ask what to do with it. Beyond that, however, the episode induced me to opt for Greek, a decision which, I suppose, shaped the course of my life.

On Sunday mornings we attended roll-call before going to church. Each boy would show up in his black jacket and striped trousers, wearing a bowler hat. In the junior house this ludicrous headgear was never treated with any respect. One manoeuvre was to sneak up behind, grab the rim of your victim's hat on each side and force it down over his ears. Another was to bash the crown in from above. As a result, although it was worn only once a week, a bowler rarely lasted more than one session. Before its final disintegration it was often used for touch rugger. After roll-call we dispersed, some going down University Road to the Methodist or Presbyterian churches, others up Lisburn Road to the Church of Ireland. The direction was symbolic, for the Church of Ireland's building had obvious links with the middle ages. The vicar, appropriately named Deane, was a rather severe intellectual-looking man, with very correct diction. He rarely preached for more than twenty minutes, and his sermons were lucid, well-constructed, pieces informing or reminding the congregation about some aspect of the faith. The emotion came from the service. At evensong, the dim lights and shadows, the pillars and pointed arches, the muted colours of the stained glass – all produced a feeling which was as close as a teenager could get to reverence. 'Lighten our darkness, we beseech thee, O Lord; and by thy great mercy defend us from all perils and dangers of this night.' The words were centuries old, but they spoke to people who, after the spring of 1941, were genuinely anxious about what the darkness might hold. And the voice, which intoned the prayers without individual inflections, sounded like the voice of the church itself. Down in the Methodist church the scene was very different. As they entered, the boys were their everyday selves. ('Hey, Beaver, can you lend us a penny? Otherwise I'll have to sell a dummy.') They filed into the school's pews at the back of the balcony, and as they leant forward to pray they were confronted, as in some tribal meeting-place, with the carvings of earlier generations. I remember recognizing with a shock the name S.P. Mercier, gouged in one-inch letters. (Mr Mercier was a much-respected member of the church in Clontarf.) The minister was the Rev. J. Wesley

Roddie, a jolly man who always preached for more than half an hour, but got away with it because he spoke in a direct intimate style and included jokes and stories. The atmosphere was not so much of reverence as of cheerful good-fellowship. This was enhanced by Mr Roddie's talents as an impresario. Outside the church there would be a large poster, saying something like: 'NEXT SUNDAY: SPECIAL VISIT OF THE RAF CHOIR, WITH SOLOIST GUNNER STEWART JONES.' This sensible, non-conformist approach was doubtless as valid as Mr Deane's. But the contrast explains why, before we split up after roll-call, a boy would turn to his friend and say, 'Where are you going, mass or music-hall?' If you wanted to avoid both ends of the spectrum, you said 'I'm for the pressbuttons'.

Scripture was well taught, and no attempt was made to push anyone in the direction of Methodism. Granted, on one occasion the Rev. Alec MacRae visited the boarders and tried to persuade everyone to sign the pledge. But this mistake was not repeated. Again, though we heard sermons from time to time which implied that each of us ought sooner or later to undergo a conversion like that of St Paul, the chaplain, Eric Gallagher, was far too sensible to regard that kind of experience as the norm. The main shortcoming of Methodism, at least at that time and place, was that its view of moral decisions did not seem to correspond with one's own experience. By this I mean that almost every preacher I heard would concentrate on the will: pray for help, nerve yourself, and then do the right thing. As we all know, that kind of situation does occur; but more common, surely, is the case where one cannot decide what the right thing is. Praying for guidance and searching one's conscience may, indeed, produce a decision; but it will only be the least bad decision, which is not how the minister would have described it. (I speak of Methodism here, because it was what I knew best. I doubt if any other denomination would have been very different.)

One morning, when I was about thirteen and a half, I woke up with a sharp pain. After breakfast I went to the san to see Nurse Quinton. She looked at me with cold blue eyes under her auburn hair. 'Pain in the tummy, you say? Hm. You wouldn't by any chance have an exam today?' 'No, nurse.' 'Well, swallow that and go upstairs and lie down.' By now I could hardly get up the stairs, and finished on my hands and knees. In the early afternoon Dr Smylie arrived. He pressed very gently on my stomach and then suddenly let go. I gave a yell and almost shot out of the bed. Twenty minutes later he was back. 'I've arranged for you to go into the Musgrave Clinic. Mr Purse will operate on you this evening.' Nurse Quinton added 'You've a wee appendix.' So that was it. After about an hour a couple of older boys came in with my pyjamas and dressing-gown. I told them what I knew. 'Barny Purse!' exclaimed one of them. 'He's *famous*. In the last war he used to operate on the men in the trenches. Sometimes he'd take a leg off without any anaesthetic!' With these cheerful thoughts in mind I was carried down to an ambulance. Much later, as I drifted slowly back to consciousness, I saw a nurse's smiling face. 'You're a lucky boy,' she said. 'Another hour and you'd have burst.'

On Tuesday 15 April 1941, when the school was on holiday, Belfast had its first air raid, a horrifying experience in which 745 people were killed and over 1600 injured. No city in Britain, it seems, except for London, suffered so heavily in a single attack.[2] Reports about that night were still fresh when the school re-opened. The Germans must have mistaken the Cavehill Water-works for the docks; the area between York Road and the Antrim Road had been levelled; fire-fighting apparatus had proved quite inadequate;[3] some brigades from Dublin had actually come up to help. The question now was, 'Has the Luftwaffe finished with us, or is there more to come?' The answer was given on the night of Sunday 4 May. About midnight the sirens began to wail and we all trooped down to the basement, which had been reinforced with thick wooden beams and fitted out with bunks. Instead of the all-clear sounding an hour later, as usually happened, an anti-aircraft battery opened up from somewhere close by. It was soon joined by others; then came the noise of exploding bombs, and before long one could hardly distinguish one kind of sound from another. Instead of lying in our bunks we gathered in the kitchen and sat talking in a desultory way. There was no tea and no gramophone. During a lull, a senior boy came in wearing a tin hat. He said it was a moonlit night, but that, in addition, there was an ominous glow over the city. He threw onto the table a few bits of shrapnel that he had picked up in the quad, and then left. Apprehension closed in as we tried not to think of what was happening. After several hours the all-clear sounded and we went back upstairs. This second raid turned out to have been far more accurate. Harland and Wolff's shipyard and Short and Harland's aircraft factory were both seriously damaged. Civilian deaths were fewer, but the total (150) was still appalling enough. According to the official German report, 204 bombers dropped 218.5 metric tons of bombs, including 95,922 incendiaries.[4] No source that I have seen (English or German) mentions any German losses.

Next day Bob Huntley, a master whom I knew very well, said, 'Look, there's no school this morning. A group of staff are organizing a messenger-service of senior boys, and I want to see the conditions for myself.' So we walked down towards the centre at about 10 a.m. Long before we reached the stricken area we smelt a pungent mixture of charred wood and filth. Fragments of material were still floating in the air. Nearer the docks, where most of the bombs had fallen, streets were cordoned off. But we could see that many houses had been wrecked. At intervals huge piles of rubble blocked the roadway, and ARP workers were still moving around. In this part, as far as I could tell, the fires had all been put out. Hose-pipes, however, still snaked all over the ground. Some were punctured here and there, sending thin jets of water shooting into the air. Everywhere streets and pavements were soaking. From time to time a strange sight would come into view, like an armchair which had been hurled into the air and had come to rest on the telephone wires. As we took in the scenes of chaos and devastation, I felt a perverse sense of relief. For if Liverpool, Bristol, Hull and a score of other cities were all being bombed, it was almost a matter of shame that, up to a few weeks ago, Belfast had been spared. At least the city had now been recognized as part of the conflict. Yet at the same time I knew there was something spurious about this pride, won as it was at the expense of the dead and injured and homeless. So far, we ourselves had lost nothing.

It was clear that as the war continued the senior boys would be joining the forces. Already the death of 'Buster' Colhoun had been announced at assembly. His record for the shot had stood for many years, and he was captain of the Ulster schools' Fifteen when Buddy Polden and Tommy Headon had played for Leinster.

Kenneth Holmes had also been killed. He cannot have been more than nineteen or twenty; for I remembered him hurdling at the school sports. Now, therefore, to give preliminary training, a unit of the Army Cadet Force (M Company) was started. Though the purpose was grimly serious, the first weeks of the unit were not without humour. At the first parade an untidy rabble fell in, to be addressed by our Commanding Officer, Mr W.H. Mol, who held the rank of Captain. Five other teachers, all Lieutenants, stood beside him. As we had no weapons or uniforms, the only sign that we were on parade was the fact that all three buttons were fastened on the jacket of Mr Mol's blue suit. He explained that we were a cadet unit of the Royal Ulster Rifles (motto: *Quis separabit?*); that we would be trained in parade-ground drill (i.e. square-bashing), map-reading, judging distance, searching ground, and the use of weapons; all being well, within the next two years we should have obtained War Certificate A. During the vacations we would be expected to attend army camps where we would be trained by regular NCO's. Finally, we were to remember that we would be brought into comparison with other companies; so it was up to us to maintain the reputation of the school.

War Certificate A might seem a long way off, but boots had to be got at once. A few weeks later, several large hampers arrived containing uniforms. Trousers and blouses had been squashed flat, as though by a giant press. They were all just slightly damp, and when peeled apart gave out a strong smell of chlorine. We selected items which seemed to be more or less the right size, and then took them away to sew on badges of identification. The next thing to arrive was a consignment of rifles – or rather carbines, for the weapons had last been used in the Boer war. They couldn't be fired, and were meant only for drill. Still, they were the right size for *us*, and it was kindly observed that in their day they were probably an advance on the musket. Two senior boys were now appointed NCO's. Both were well liked and effective, but they offered rather different role models. Barry Pinion, medium-sized, with black floppy hair, played jazz piano and enjoyed an occasional fag. Gerry Murphy, tall and straight, was a fellow of great charm and integrity who was later capped for Ireland at full back and later still became the Queen's Chaplain at Sandringham.

For some of our instruction we would troop into the Botanic Gardens, which were part of a large park sloping down to the Lagan. Few people went there on weekdays, and on Sundays, when the citizens would have been free to use it, the gates were sternly locked. For weapon training we used the OTC building in Queen's University which contained a rifle range. Rifles were cleaned with a piece of material called a 'four by two'. This was drawn through the barrel by a cord, which was kept in a little chamber in the butt. The instructor's procedure for cleaning rifles therefore ran 'open your butt-trap and take out your pull-through' – a sequence which the squad found irresistibly comic. I attended four camps in all, at Rockport, Holywood, McGilligan Strand, and Warrenpoint, and I recall them all without affection. Blankets had to be folded precisely to within an eighth of an inch, and the Nissen hut had to be swept again and again even when it was clear that the concrete floor was actually *generating* dust. After meals you dipped your tin plate and cutlery in two large drums of hot water behind the cookhouse, which would have been all right if the people in front had first scraped off the remains of their food. Once or twice you were given a shovel and detailed to clean out the latrines. For that sickening task once was too often, even if all the receptacles had been accurately positioned. As it was, some people could only bear to do the job after donning their gas masks. Then there were the route marches, boring and exhausting affairs which, like real troops from Britain to Burma, we tried to enliven by singing about the Nazi leaders and their genital defects to the tune of Col. Bogey. Another marching song had to do with a seduction in ten stages, each punctuated with a refrain beginning 'roll me over, lay me down, and do it again'. All of which our Chaplain, who was marching behind us, wisely failed to hear. Back in camp we would go to sing-songs and impromptu concerts, which (since they were provided by ourselves) were of a fairly dismal standard, but prevented us from sinking into a state of clinical depression.

It was sometimes said in favour of camp that you came across people of a kind that you wouldn't otherwise have met. This was true. One summer evening when I was watching cricket with the MO, I noticed him place one hand on his lower abdomen and tap it with the fingers of the other. 'If you listen carefully,' he said, 'you can tell from the sound whether you need to go for a pee.' Scientifically, the method sounded plausible enough, but one wondered if it was really necessary. At one of the camps our squad's instructor was Sergeant-Major Caughey. I suppose he was only about thirty-five, but he was a hard-bitten veteran who had come through several years of active service with the infantry. We all admired him, and would have followed him anywhere. One morning the Colonel appeared, complete with cane and white breeches. Standing at the back of the squad I thought I heard Caughey say 'Here comes this broccoli-bred bastard'. Someone objected 'But he's a Field Officer, isn't he?' 'He is. But you know what we say when we hear someone's got a commission? We say he's stupid enough to be a general.' I saw the point of that all right, but I did wonder for some time why eating broccoli should be a matter for reproach.

The Colonel came wandering over, and when the formalities were done he said, 'Well then, I hope you're all enjoying kemp!' 'Hum, yum, rhubarb rhubarb.' 'Jolly good. What's the grub like?' Brief silence; then a diplomat spoke, 'Rather better than school, sir.' '*Jolly* good.' Then, becoming more serious, 'Ahem. Look here … I want you chaps to know that … well … you're most *frightfully* important. You see … well … dammit, old chaps like Col. Gibbon and me … we've had our day.' (Col. Gibbon was Headmaster of Campbell College.) 'And you … well, to put it in a nutshell, you're the chaps who are going to … going to be … well, you're going to be the *chaps*, you see. Of course I don't suppose this war's going to last forever … Once we've got Jerry on the run, why then … But, you know, even in peacetime the army's no bad thing. Healthy life … travel … lots of sport …' As he droned on, it suddenly occurred to me, good Lord, here's a man who actually *likes* soldiering.

From time to time M Company had to take part in huge public parades. On such occasions it seemed that every organization that could boast a uniform had sent a detachment. As well as navy, army and air force (both genders), one had nurses and firemen, land-girls and air-raid wardens; and, for all I know, bus-drivers and postmen. But the best marchers were always the Royal Ulster Constabulary. They would choose men of about six foot one, and then drill them until, with their white gloves and high black caps, they presented a miracle of line and movement. M Company was not up to that standard. At the Wings for Victory parade, which involved marching past a saluting-base in front of the City Hall, we formed up in good time somewhere behind the Technical College. Our CO was a highly accurate scholar and an efficient organizer; but when it came to marching he tended to concentrate too hard, instead of letting instinct guide him. This led to problems of co-ordination, which he dealt with by marching very slowly and restricting the swing of his arms to a short arc in front of his body where he could, as it were, keep an eye on them. This didn't matter too much as we moved out into the cheering, flag-waving crowd. But farther ahead, beside the saluting-base, stood the band of the Royal Ulster Rifles – a regiment with the fast marching pace of 140. As we came into view, the band struck up the regimental march. This led to a dramatic increase in pace, and people had to change step farther down the line. Suddenly a woman's voice came out of the crowd, which was only a yard away on each side of our column, 'May Gawd, you'd think thon man was dhravin' a kyar!' Then, on the word of command, we jerked our heads round to the right and hurried past the saluting base, looking, no doubt, like a clip from an early movie. So, for about four years, we went through the hoops, poring over maps, crawling along ditches, unjamming Bren guns, and bellowing at people across parade grounds. We were assured that, in addition to replenishing the allied forces, the training was doing us good. Perhaps it was. Nevertheless, except for a few madheads, we fervently hoped it would all be over before our turn came. *Playing* at war was bad enough.

On 29 February 1940 two senior girls stopped me in the main corridor. One said 'Do you know what year this is?' 'Nineteen-forty,' I answered. 'Ah yes, but 1940 is a *leap*-year. And in *leap*-years, on February the 29th, girls propose to boys.' 'Oh?' I said, feeling distinctly uneasy. 'Yes. So what I want to know is, will you marry me?' This was awful. 'I ... er ... thank you ... I'm afraid I'm late for geography ... have to hurry.' 'Oh that's *too* bad; I'm *so* sorry. Perhaps four years from now?' As I ran off, I heard their laughter. 'That's a tanner you owe me, Helen!' Needless to say, in a large co-educational school, innocence did not survive very long

– innocence, that is, in a purely theoretical sense. Our Victorian ancestors, we are told, were excited by the glimpse of a well-turned ankle. In the 1940s, schoolgirls' legs were visible to the top of the knee-cap (higher if you were lucky). The fact that they were encased in heavy black stockings did little to diminish their attraction. Nor did the plain utility gym-slip succeed in neutralizing our interest. In the case of the first hockey XI, a white strip tacked round the hem served only to call attention to that all-important boundary which divided what might be from what might not be seen. When the girl boarders took up residence in a wing of our building, and appeared at meal-times in the dining-hall, gossip and speculation redoubled. Nevertheless, they still had separate tables from ours, and anything like a private conversation was hard to contrive. So the occasional dance or other social event was eagerly awaited.

Form dances, for day pupils and boarders combined, were a recent innovation. When the idea was first proposed by a group of liberal-minded teachers, they were told that the governors would never allow it. So they advertised a sixth-form party and invited along the Chairman. Then a teacher announced that he and the gym mistress would now demonstrate a musical walk. They started with a military two-step, and before long the floor was full of couples charging round to Blaze Away. The Chairman, a frail and guileless old gentleman, said the musical walk was a very cheerful idea, 'and good exercise too', and he left shortly after. The door was now open for St Bernard, Velita, and Victory waltzes; and the following year all the senior forms were doing fox-trots and quicksteps. Our friends on the staff could certainly have defended such functions to the governors as part of our social education. None of us would have used such pompous language. We just thought the dances were excellent fun, with an occasional dash of glamour and romance; and certain tunes ('The Skaters' Waltz', 'Cherokee', 'Darktown Strutters' Ball') will always bring them back.

It was at a fifth-form dance that I met a delightful girl, whom I shall call Jane. After one or two Sunday afternoon walks on Cavehill, I devised what seemed a daring and ingenious ploy. At the end of the Easter vacation, I would take the train to Belfast as usual, but instead of going straight to school I would ask Jane to meet me and we would go to a cinema. It worked out splendidly. Jane arrived wearing a white overcoat with a little shamrock brooch that I had given her in the lapel, and we walked down Great Victoria Street to the Ritz, where the newly released *Casablanca* was being shown. In that exotic city, peopled by some memorably seedy villains, the story of menace and desperation unfolds. At the end Rick, the apparently cynical night-club owner, contrives the escape of a resistance fighter and of a girl whom they both love – an act of self-abnegation which shows that (in a rather different sense from that suggested by the song) 'the fundamental things apply'. There is no pious moralizing. The nearest thing to an ethical explanation comes when Bogart says to Bergman, 'The problems of three little people don't amount to a hill of beans in this crazy world.' True, we are half prepared for Rick's decision by a previous act of generosity; yet, in view of the man's character and his past record, it is not wholly predictable – except, it seems, to the Chief of Police. 'I was right, Rick, you *are* a sentimentalist,' says Claude Raines, without a trace of a French accent. Unlike, say, *Mrs Miniver*, in which the attitudes to class now seem rather comic, *Casablanca* has not dated in any way that matters. In the last half century it has achieved a cult status, especially in America. (One thinks of Woody Allen's *Play it Again, Sam*.) Yet it will always retain a special poignancy for people who remember the 1940s. And amongst those there must be a few who associate it with the first time they took a girl to the pictures.

In the boarding department as a whole, all the talk and the affectionate letters (secretly conveyed) led to little in the way of sexual behaviour. The girls were carefully supervised, so the boys tended to rely on the day-girls for their adventures. Even then, encounters were usually limited to 'necking sessions' in the back row of the Majestic and the Regal on a Saturday afternoon. On special occasions we were given free leave, which meant that we could spend the night away from school, provided we gave the name and address of our hosts. So, from time to time, one made an arrangement with a day-boy's kindly parents and then went out dancing. Such plans did not always succeed. Once a friend of mine spent the evening with a girl but failed to arrange accommodation. He was climbing over a wall, with the intention of stealing quietly into his bed, when he had the ill luck to be caught. 'McKeown, what on *earth* are you doing here at this time of night?' McKeown, speaking from the top of the wall, 'Oh, hello sir ... I'm on free leave, and I was just ... er ... coming back to fetch my pyjamas.' Serious temptations were rare. Once, when we were nearly eighteen, a friend and I received an explicit invitation from two sixth-form girls whose parents were out of town. We were, of course, flattered and interested; but in the end we thought up some pretext which would save everybody's face, and declined. Our motives overlapped but were not identical. All brands of Christianity, Methodism included, were then unambiguous about such matters: extra-marital sex was a sin. Our upbringing had made the point equally clear. Such factors may well have weighed more heavily with my friend, who was quite religious. My own decision was prompted rather by fear – fear of disgrace and expulsion, and, far worse than that, fear of making the girl pregnant. Of course we had been told about so-called 'FLs', but I never heard of anyone who had the nerve to walk into a chemist's in his school uniform and ask the (usually) female assistant for a packet of contraceptives. And anyhow the things were said to be not 100 per cent reliable. As for the 'safe period', that was known to be an illusion. So, in a rather technical sense, our innocence was preserved.

Permissiveness, then, was unheard of in the Methodist College. (I doubt in fact if the word acquired its present connotations before the 1960s.) Yet the presence of the girls ensured that the school's orientation was decidedly heterosexual. Granted, one or two of the staff had homosexual tendencies, but tendencies are not the same as behaviour. Amongst the boys in the boarding department, homosexuality was rare, mild, and nearly always transitory. The contrast here with traditional single-sex institutions (e.g. boys' public schools, some branches of the navy, and prisons) supports the commonsense view that homosexuality is not wholly a matter of genes; environment may also be a factor. Once one goes beyond this banal generalization and tries to study how a homosexual should be defined, how many are genetically determined, how many are temporarily influenced by an institution and then revert to heterosexual behaviour, how many are bisexual, and so on, one enters a jungle of statistics. Then there are questions of interpretation. How reliable is the sample (i.e. are they telling the truth)? How representative is the sample? Were the questions accurately framed? What can be inferred from the answers? Statistical jungles have other dangers too. During one of the earliest surveys, and certainly the most famous, Mrs Kinsey told an interviewer 'I don't see too much of Alfred these days since he's gotten so interested in sex.'

Things have probably changed in the last half century, but at Methodist College in the 1940s reading was passively discouraged. Except at lunch-hour once or twice a week, the library (being at the girls' end of the school) was out of bounds. The books were locked away in high cases, so that browsing was impossible. And even if the books had been accessible, no time or place was set aside for reading them. This rather dismal state of affairs was mitigated by two factors. The first (from which I benefited more than most) was the presence of a teacher who moved into residence about 1941. This was Bob Huntley, whose father had come to the shipyard in Belfast in the 1920s because of the situation in Jarrow. Bob had started a degree in Queen's University, but had withdrawn for financial reasons and taken a teacher training course at Stranmillis. He was an excellent teacher, particularly of the less able – he got me through both Junior and Senior grade in elementary maths. Since maths teachers, then as now, were in short supply, he never had a chance to teach his favourite subject, which was English literature. But he maintained a lively interest in the arts, and I must have absorbed a certain amount by attending plays, films and concerts in his company and then arguing about them afterwards. Though he rather disliked sport, Bob was an energetic officer in the cadet force, and along with one of the mistresses he took boys and girls youth-hostelling in the Mournes and the Trossacks. After some years he was appointed Head of the Junior School, but sadly he died of lung cancer while still in his fifties. As I think of him now, I can see him with his gold-coloured hair and rather high colour, standing before the class with a small vein throbbing in his left temple (a sure warning that it was time to stop fooling around); or sitting at the end of the front row in the Hippodrome and gazing up sideways through the smoke of a thousand cigarettes at Laughton's *Hunchback of Notre Dame* (distortion distorted); or huddled, with a bilious face, on the deck of a cattle-boat as it pitched and rolled through the darkness towards the mouth of the Clyde. Thanks to him, I heard the soprano Joan Cross and dined with the mezzo Anna Pollack (both visiting with Sadlers Wells); met radio actors like James Boyce and Cicely Matthews; and listened to the talk of various regular colonels. Sometimes he would be angry. One December, for in-stance, bearing in mind that for some reason his school nickname was 'Bumf', I sent him a sheet of toilet paper instead of a Christmas card. Unfortunately the envelope was opened by his mother, who was shocked at the coarseness of her son's young friend. At other times I failed to allow for his sensitivity about questions of class. Thus, when I mimicked a regular sergeant, who came to take the cadets for gym and kept referring to a sand-bag as 'a bague o'sond', Bob said 'How *dare* you make fun of him! Don't you real-ize it's a *tragedy* that anyone should talk like that?' He hated a yellow pullover which I occasionally wore, because he associated such a garment with vulgar yobbos. And once he took offence when, after visiting his house, I remarked that at home we drank cocoa made with milk. '*Your* family may assume that milk is always available; mine doesn't.' Usually we got on very well, but in retro-spect it is clear that I gained far more from our friendship than he.

The other, more general factor that provided some education outside class was the formation of various societies about 1943 – societies for debating, music-appreciation, drama, and so on. One of the earliest debates was on Éire's neutrality, in which for obvi-ous reasons I was told to defend de Valera's position. Since none of us had any experience in debating, the evening produced no rhetorical masterpieces, but I remember using the following, rather familiar, arguments: (1) England only wanted Éire to enter the war so that she could use the Atlantic ports; those ports had been formally handed over to Éire in 1938, so England had no legal right to claim them. (2) Although neutrality denied the allies the use of the ports, it absolved England from having to defend a country which had no navy or air force, and it allowed many thou-sands of Irishmen to join the allies as volunteers. Lord Donegal, from whom I had obtained a letter, estimated the total at about 38,000. (This is a conservative figure, but larger totals are insecure.)[5] (3) Centuries of domination had left a legacy of anti-British feeling. If Éire entered the war, the civil strife which had ended only twenty years before would probably break out again; and that would only damage the allied cause. (4) In the first world war huge numbers from Southern Ireland had fought for Britain in the expectation that the promise of independence would be fulfilled. In the event, England had succumbed to Ulster pressure and imposed partition. The senior housemaster, Ronnie Marshall, weighed in on my side with two sly provocative points: (1) Northern Ireland had no moral right to criticize Éire, since there was no conscription *either* side of the border. (2) The USA had stayed out of the war until it was attacked, and countries like Sweden and Switzerland had remained neutral without incurring obloquy. So why criticize Éire? The reader will have his own opinion about the relative cogency of these arguments. One need hardly add that on the night my side of the house was heavily defeated. At the time, of course, we were all aware of the terrible losses in the Atlantic. It was admitted that these losses were partly due to Éire's refusal to cede the ports (an act which would, of course, have meant the end of neutrality). What was not known, and what one learned with astonishment many years later, was the fact that until 1943 the Germans were able to read the British naval codes.[6] So it seems that British carelessness was as much to blame as Irish intransigence. This point is worth making in view of the rightly admired and widely proclaimed successes of the British cryptographers.[7]

In my last year at school the dramatic society's main undertaking was a production of Aeschylus' *Agamemnon* in Gilbert Murray's translation. This play, the first of the trilogy known as the *Oresteia*, enacts the return of Agamemnon from Troy along with the prophetess Cassandra, his captured slave. Queen Clytemnestra already hates him for sacrificing their daughter Iphigeneia. So, in conjunction with her lover Aegisthus, she plots his murder. In due course Agamemnon arrives, steps down from his chariot, and walks into the palace over a purple carpet, thus demonstrating his hybris. That is the last time we see him alive, though we hear his cry of agony as he is murdered in his bath. In the other two plays Orestes avenges the death of his father by killing Clytemnestra, and is in turn pursued by the Furies. He is finally acquitted at a trial where Athena casts the deciding vote. This court, which foreshadows the establishment of a homicide court in Athens, breaks the chain of retaliatory murders and thus marks a significant step in the emergence of Greek civilization. Even without the other two plays, *Agamemnon* is a large and complex work, involving all the challenges of *Macbeth*, plus choral music and movement. Yet, if its status as one of the world's great dramas is to be upheld, it must from time to time be produced, even if the only people willing to take the risk are a handful of school teachers and their pupils.

The initial idea, it must be acknowledged, came from Bos, who got permission from Murray to use his translation, and then edited out some of the obscurities and preciosities. He also cleaned one or two passages up. For example, the chorus refers to Menelaus' empty bed after the departure of Helen – 'a couch, a couch empty, that was once pressed in love.' Under Bos's subtle hand this became 'a couch, a couch empty, that was once blessed with love.' Ernie Stoneley was then persuaded to write music for the choral odes. He did a splendid job, though at the start one or two minor misunderstandings had to be removed. When he was rehearsing with the chorus an ode which described the pursuit of Helen and Paris's ship, he sang '... came the hunters in a flood down the car-blade's viewless trail.' At that moment Bos entered the room. 'I say, Dr ... eh, what's this car-blade?' Stoneley looked puzzled. 'Here, Dr ... eh, let me see the script. Ach, for heaven's sake, the word is *oar*-blade.' Stoneley's face creased in good-humoured mortification. 'Well, thank you Mr Bullick. I did *wonder*.' Meanwhile Bos was half-way out the door muttering '*car*-blade, indeed!'

Bob Huntley agreed to produce the play, with the assistance of one or two colleagues. Casting was not by invitation, or consultation, but by decree: 'You will be Agamemnon, you Clytemnestra', and so on; and then (to me) 'you're the chorus-leader.' So that was that. Colleagues were then enlisted to look after set, props, lighting, and costumes; others saw to the programmes and publicity; others undertook to coach us in choral speaking and movement. Luckily no fancy manoeuvres were required, since we were supposed to be a group of Argive elders. The king's chariot caused a temporary problem, but Bos was equal to it. 'I personally have arranged for the hire of a porter's trolley from the Great Northern Railway'. In the event, the college carpenter, Jimmy Kelly, used only the wheels and the axle, building a magnificent new super-structure with a single pole, so that the vehicle could be hauled on stage by a quartet of attendants. The whole chariot was then given a coat of gilt paint and decorated with a Greek key pattern.

Even at the dress rehearsal there were a few anxious moments. At one point a character was supposed to speak words of comfort – 'a moment's respite brings of hope a ray'. This came out, carefully articulated, as 'a moment's respite brings a rope of hay'. Again, as he stood in his chariot and began to move towards the stage, Agamemnon suddenly realized that he wasn't going to get through the door with his helmet on. As he saw the lintel coming at him he clutched his helmet, ducked like a pugilist, and then resumed his arrogant mien as he was drawn onto the stage. That had to be put right. But when the time came, the play was staged on three suc-cessive evenings and proved an enormous success. Aeschylus came across $2^{1}/_{2}$ millennia, triumphing over Murray's Swinburnian translation, Stoneley's Edwardian music, and the actors' all too numerous limitations. The audience responded warmly and even the critics were generous. The performers themselves, however, were only dimly aware of the effect that was being created. Pre-sumably an experienced actor can sense an audience's mood and adjust his timing and pointing accordingly. But we were concen-trating so hard on coming in on the right beat, singing in tune, and getting the words right that we were barely conscious of what was happening beyond the footlights. Crises on stage were a dif-ferent matter. On the first night Dr Stoneley said 'Mr Clarence Bailey (entomology and botany) will be stationed in the orchestra pit, just to give you complete confidence; he will bring you in on the right beat'. As we stood in line across the front of the stage, I saw old Buggy Bailey's bald head gleaming in the half-light; when it came to the second part of the opening chorus, we knew we had to enter at the beginning of the third bar with 'We saw the avengers go that day ...' The orchestra duly played one bar 'me ray doh ray me fah me'; and then, to my horror, in came Buggy's quavering tenor '... we saw the avengers ...' Luckily no one came in with him, and his voice trailed off. At the next two performances the poor man sat in the same place but never uttered another note. On the second night Clytemnestra advanced to put a circular crown (without a top) on the kneeling Aegisthus' head. Suddenly a vigilant member of the chorus hissed 'Mary, the crown's upside down!' Without a moment's pause she turned the crown over in the act of placing it in position. Huge relief all round. Otherwise it would have come down over Aegisthus' eyes, making him look like a tipsy tennis player. Finally, on the last night (these things happen in threes), I saw from the tail of my eye a spear begin to sway; then a shield crashed onto the stage, followed closely by its owner. The soldier's comrades rested their weapons against the palace wall and manhandled the body into the wings. Members of the audience were kind enough to say that they had assumed it was all part of the plot and that the man had been overcome by the pathos of Cassandra's speech. After it was all over, Bob Huntley said 'You know we should keep all this stuff and use it as a basis for a collection of costumes and props. That chariot-top, for instance, might well turn in handy.' Bos immediately intervened. 'Aye, but hold on there now, Mr ... eh; you see, that chariot is the property of the Great Northern Railway.'

Like other Protestant schools in Northern Ireland, Methody played rugger; colours: dark blue jersey and shorts, blue and white striped stockings. Ground: Pirrie Park, near to Ravenhill and having the same muscle-wrenching turf. Coach: Mr Alastair Clarke, a chemistry teacher from Edinburgh who, twenty years before, had been a champion hurdler and a fast wing three-quarter. He was a thin, medium-sized man with black wavy hair and a lined, rather sallow face. He also had sloping shoulders which, when clothed in a brown sports coat, reminded the more discerning of a bottle of hock. Though always on the point of giving up, he smoked about forty cigarettes a day. As a result his rather satirical laughter usually ended in a fit of coughing. (In those days people didn't recognize what that might imply.) Occasionally we would have to travel to Foyle College (Derry), Campbell (Portrush), or Portora (Enniskillen), returning in a dismal blacked-out carriage with a small shaft of bluish light coming from the middle of the roof. There was little to do other than sing or doze, though one or two of our more advanced team-mates would prowl up and down the darkened train, which always carried service personnel, in the hope of finding a compliant member of the ATS. When we first saw the Northern Counties Hotel in Port-rush, to which Campbell College had been evacuated, I thought, 'This is the most luxurious place that I've ever changed in.' Then, as we climbed successive flights of stairs, and moved farther to the back of the building, the quality of carpet deteriorated; linoleum appeared; and the room where we actually changed had bare boards – just like our own pavilion.

On an old map, which I saw much later, Portora's playing-fields were marked as a lake. Shortly before the war a new drainage scheme had produced a low-lying, but beautifully even surface. Unfortunately the authorities decided to raise the level of Lough Erne in order to make it more suitable for flying-boats; whereupon the water flowed back down the drainage channels. The result was a soggy field with a deep dyke just beyond the touchline. When we played there in the winter of 1945, Gerry Murphy, who had come charging across the field to head off an attack, disappeared into the dyke. He emerged to shouts of 'Don't forget the diver!' (a catch-phrase from 'Itma', Tommy Handley's show). You can always rely on your friends for sympathy. Later on, as the train did not leave for another forty minutes, I wandered down to the lake, where an apparently derelict Sunderland was floating just off shore. With the aid of a small dinghy I got out to it and clambered aboard. After looking round the inside I managed, with some contortions, to climb up into the gun-turret. The seat, which had been folded back to allow access, clicked into place, and I settled down to destroy marauding Messerschmidts. Shortly after, I prepared to leave; but try as I would, I couldn't release the catch on the seat. Minutes ticked by as I pushed and pulled and squeezed. I began to be seriously worried; the train would be leaving, and it was getting dark. Macabre headlines from the local paper came into my mind: 'Skeleton discovered in floating hulk', 'Who was the phantom gunner?' Then suddenly, and inexplicably, the catch opened and I was out. Derisive cheers greeted me as I ran across the platform. 'Was she as good as all that?' 'Bully old Simeon!' Blast them anyway. 'Simeon' was a nickname, or rather the corruption of a nickname, which had boomeranged on me. I had once addressed my out-half and friend Chuck Evans as 'Simian', because he was even shorter and squatter than myself. The name stuck, but not to him. I carried it through my last two years at school.

At the end of the 1943–4 season, when I was sixteen, I was brought onto the first fifteen as scrum-half. One of the last fixtures was against Belfast Royal Academy at their ground on Cave Hill. Before we took the field, Alastair Clarke included something quite unusual in his pep-talk, for he rarely mentioned any of the opposition by name. 'Now look here – you two wing-forwards, and you, stand-off. This fellow Kyle is playing today. A fine footballer in my opinion. We don't want to see him sprinting down the middle. So just make sure that when the ball goes to him you arrive at the same time!' With that, the corners of his mouth went down, his eyes opened wide, and with a prefatory 'yes!' he emitted one of his sardonic laughs. It is possible, in fact, that Jack Kyle wasn't given much room that day, for one of our wing forwards was the captain, Ewart Bell, who later played for Ireland, and *much* later ended up with a knighthood as head of Northern Ireland's civil service. But if Jack Kyle *was* frustrated, he will have taken it phlegmatically; for he was the most even-tempered and the least conceited of men. In Dublin a few years later, at a dance in the Metropole, I saw him listening with unfeigned politeness to a slightly drunken member of Wanderers' thirds, who was explaining what the great out-half should have done to prevent Ireland losing to France that afternoon.

In 1945 we played Belvedere College for the first time at Pirrie Park. The previous year Alastair Clarke and a colleague had been royally entertained by the Jesuits when the team visited Dublin. So a few days before the match he said, 'Look here, Rudd, why don't you wander along and have a word with the good lady who does the catering at Downey House [the prep. school in Pirrie Park]. Tell her what's happening, and ask if she'd be kind enough to give us all tea – pies, sausage rolls, sandwiches – that sort of thing – anything she can lay her hands on.' Then the corners of the mouth went down. 'They gave us an excellent time in Dublin, and it wouldn't do to let our Roman brethren surpass us in Christian charity!' The punch-line culminated in the usual spasm. That year

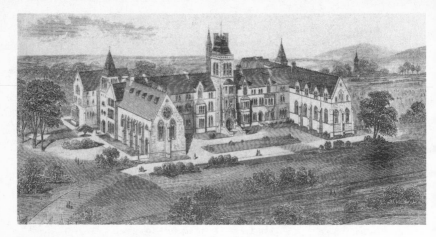

The Methodist College, Malone Road, Belfast, in 1868 (from an engraving by Marcus Ward).

Ulster Schools XV *vs* Leinster Schools XV at Ravenhill, 1946.
Back row, l. to r.: Mr Morgan (referee), Crossey, Bredin, Elliott, Stevenson, Doherty, Morrow, Warke, Beringer. *Front*: Thompson, Maguire, McDowell, Rudd, Bridges, Boston, Evans.

our team qualified to meet Inst (Royal Belfast Academical Institution) in the final of the Ulster Schools' Cup, an event which always generated intense excitement. In previous years I had watched games in which Coleraine and Portora had taken part; the crowds had been enormous, and one was tempted to believe the report that the towns of Coleraine and Enniskillen had closed down for the day. Yet some people thought the whole thing was unwise. Col. Gibbon had taken Campbell College out of the competition on the grounds that it involved too much publicity and imposed too much strain on the boys. Rugby, after all, was only a game; better to keep it in perspective. Moreover, the strength of a team depended on the number of heavy forwards and fast backs that the school could muster, and that in turn loaded the dice heavily in favour of the large city institutions. These were serious points, and I am now half inclined to agree with Col. Gibbon. However, none of us thought that way at the time, and although Methody had not enjoyed an especially good season and was not expected to win, we prepared to do battle. In the changing-room under the grandstand the atmosphere was tense. Our mouths were dry as we put on our boots amid the smell of embrocation. 'Remember now, don't pay the slightest attention to the crowd. *They*'re not playing. They're only there to make a noise.' So said Alastair Clarke, rightly. But nothing prepared us for the deafening roar that went up when the teams ran onto the pitch. We could hardly hear the ref's whistle or our captain's voice, and much of the game was played in a kind of daze. No doubt professional footballers are used to such conditions, but it was all new to us, and I for one didn't like it. In the end we were beaten as expected, and I left the ground with some relief, and in quite good spirits. The season finished with the inter-provincial match against Leinster at Lansdowne Road. This was altogether more fun. Since a province means so much less than a school, there was no awful feeling of responsibility; the crowd was pleasantly small; the turf was good, and it was exciting to play at Lansdowne Road, where I had so often been a spectator.

In the spring of 1946 Methody was again due to meet Inst in the cup-final. This time we had a better-balanced team, and had already beaten our opponents earlier in the season, so people thought we had a fair chance of winning. But, ten days before the game, things began to go wrong. Our full-back fell ill and had to cry off. Soon after that I was taken into hospital with an infected gland, and next day our star centre, Kenneth Maguire, appeared in the next bed. We were pumped full of penicillin and discharged two days before the game, only to hear that another three-quarter had strained a leg muscle and would have to be strapped. When the time came, we took to the field with the same pandemonium as before. Chuck Evans scored first. Then, in the second half, Inst won possession from a scrum near our line. In such cases the plan was that I would take the blind side and the full-back the open side. As I went round, I suddenly realized that the Inst scrum-half was heading for the line and that our full-back was not in position. Not his fault. He was a replacement and had not been briefed. Soon after, I was sure I had atoned for this lapse by crossing the Inst line. I grounded the ball, and a second later was pushed into touch. The touch-judge, Mr Billy Majury, kept his flag down and nodded to the referee to confirm the try. But the latter, who had been on the other side of the scrum and had not seen what happened, failed to consult the touch-judge and ordered a drop out. Protesting to the referee would have been unthinkable, and the game continued. By now our team-mate's leg muscle was so painful that he was a virtual passenger. Inst quite rightly seized the initiative, and scored again. So that was it. There were smiles and handshakes all round as the cup was presented to my opposite number, Freddie MacDowell. We showered, changed, and gloomily dispersed. 'Ah well,' sighed Alastair Clarke. 'There's nothing for it now but to retire to Russia!' Back in school, I shut the door of my cubicle, threw myself on the bed and, for the first time in ten years, wept.

By the day of the interprovincial my self-pity had subsided, and I sat once again in the Ravenhill dressing-room looking forward to an enjoyable game. Just before we went out, the Inst coach came over and said 'Rudd, you're captain today. Here's the ball.' This was a nice surprise, but clearly it wasn't right. So I demurred. 'But sir, surely Freddie MacDowell should be doing this.' 'No no. The matter's been decided. So just go ahead, and good luck.' There was no time to reflect on this generous gesture before we were out on the field. Whatever he may have felt, Freddie never showed the slightest resentment. The spirit in which the match was played was illustrated in two subsequent remarks. One came from the Leinster sprinter, Louis Crowe. 'Twice, when I thought I was away, I was grassed from behind. I'm not used to that!' (This was a tribute to Kenneth Maguire, who was marking him that day.) The other came from the two hookers, who complained that, as the Leinster scrum-half came from Belfast and the Ulster scrum-half was a Dubliner, their accents caused total confusion when the ball was put in. Schools' rugger was a clean game, partly owing to the teachers' authority. In one practice-match I used a hand-trip, a trick I had just learned. The second time I did it, Alastair Clarke blew the whistle. 'Here, cut out this hand-tripping, Rudd. It's a rabbit's way of bringing a man down.' Equally, obstruction and dirty play amongst the forwards (as far as I could judge) were most uncommon. But the question of the cup competition remains. Last year Sir John Megaw, who played for Ireland in 1934 and 1938, was told by his daughter (a colleague of mine) that I was a Methody man. 'Convey my greetings,' said the judge, 'and tell him that the one painful memory of my schooldays is the defeat of my Inst team by Methody in the cup competition of 1928.' Of course schools must play each other; and someone must lose. But at eighteen should it really matter so much? Back in 1940, as petrol supplies gave out, the motor business in Dublin had collapsed. My father (now separated from my mother) eventually came north and found a job in a munitions factory, where he worked as a fitter, often on night shifts. He had a room in a lodging-house not far from the school; so quite often we would spend Sunday afternoon together and have a sort of high tea before I returned for evening church. In that period he sometimes made caustic comments on what he saw happening at work. More than once he quoted an anti-Ulster quip that was circulating at the time: 'Yes, they say they're loyal to the crown; but if you ask me, they're *more* loyal to the *half*-crown.' Then a satirical anecdote would follow; e.g. 'Did you hear about the King's visit to Short and Harland's? He said to a fitter "How many fighters have you turned out this week?" "Twenty-five, your Majesty." "Twenty-five fighters? Why, that's superb!" "Oh was it *fighters*, your Majesty? I'm sorry. I thought you said *lighters*."' These remarks worried me, partly because they went against all my preconceptions of Ulster (which was regarded in Clontarf as a bastion of loyalty), and partly because they did not seem to connect with anything that I had observed at school. I was old enough to realize that my father had suffered what is now called 'a culture shock' on the floor of the munitions factory – a harsher and uglier shock than I had received at school. He would sometimes talk of the noise and dirt and discomfort, and of something which he found particularly distasteful – the foulness of the women's language. During those same months he developed the half-conscious habit of constantly cleaning and filing his fingernails. So the severity of his reaction was to some extent personal. Yet one couldn't simply dismiss his stories of time-wasting and carelessness. Evidently the war effort was not quite as solid and whole-hearted as we had been led to believe.[8] When discussing these awkward topics, one was tempted to ascribe the ambiguities in Ulster's loyalty (defective war effort, lack of conscription) solely to the pressure of Irish nationalists supported by de Valera, and to explain the inconsistencies in Éire's neutrality (the connivance at flights across Donegal, the return of allied personnel who had landed in the Republic) solely in terms of the pressure of Ulster unionists supported by the British government. Yet such neat analyses would have been far too simple. And anyway, some people managed to make the best of things as they were.

Once, in late 1942 I think, when my father and I were looking for a meal, we enquired in a small, rather dim-looking hotel in the area of Bedford Street. The door was opened by a bald, medium-sized man with aggressive dentures, who said yes, we could have a fry; would bacon, egg, sausage and potato-bread do? We accepted at once, for such things were luxuries. We were shown into a front room with a large rectangular table. After twenty minutes or so, our plates came in, piled high with the items we had ordered. There was also plenty of home-baked bread and butter, and a large bowl of white sugar. As we set to, our host continued to hover. So, no doubt to excuse my voracity, my father said 'The lad here has to get back to Methody in time for evening service'. 'Ah Methody is it? That's a fine school. Aye, I don't hold with secular schooling. In times like these we must hold fast to religion. In fact,' he corrected himself, 'we must *always* hold fast to religion.' We mumbled assent through our bacon and eggs. 'The Bishop was saying that only this morning. He was preaching on the text "Be ye perfect, even as your Father in Heaven is perfect."' 'Not an easy task,' said my father. 'No no. That's what his Lordship was saying this morning in St Anne's. We can't do it for ourselves. We have to pray for divine grace… Aye, it was a fine sermon, and good to see such a large congregation.' 'It'll be a big place when it's finished.' 'It will surely. My name, by the way, is Brodie – George Brodie.' My father introduced us. 'Are there any visitors to Belfast these days?' 'Oh aye. Plenty of soldiers. Especially Americans. In my line of business the Americans are best. Last weekend I had to turn them away. As it was I took in fifteen. Aye, fifteen. They were sleepin' all over the place. Six of them were on the floor in here. But I didn't mind. I charged them twelve and six each.' 'Quite a lot of money,' said my father. 'Well yes, it would be for *our* boys, but not for them. No no. They're very well paid, you see.' 'Well, we must be on our way, then.' 'Bye bye and come back again.' 'Goodbye.' When we were outside, I said, 'What did he charge?' 'Six bob each.' 'Good heavens!' 'Yes, but look at what we had.' 'Hm. I wonder where he got it.' 'Quite. He must know someone *we* don't know.' We then walked up University Road, well fed but with slightly uneasy consciences.

I did see George Brodie again, but not at his hotel. The Dublin-Belfast train always stopped at Goraghwood for customs. Once, at the previous station, the corridor door slid back and in came George. He seemed to be moving rather stiffly, a fact which I put down to encroaching arthritis. He didn't recognize me, and I at once hid behind a magazine. At Goraghwood our cases were examined without incident. Then, as we puffed down the Lagan valley towards Belfast, I noticed that George's trousers had ridden up high above his socks, revealing a large expanse of long johns. But the long johns were tight and bulging, and the bulges were held in place by lengths of strong twine. So his impaired mobility was due not to arthritis, but to contraband. Granted, I had once been an accomplice, but I now paid for this with the thought that what I had eaten so greedily at his hotel had been imported in George's underclothes.

In the spring of 1941 my father got a job with the Air Ministry which put him in charge of heavy plant at a new airfield then being constructed at Millisle in the Ards Peninsula. This job, which was a lot better than standing all night beside a lathe, brought with it the use of a Vauxhall van, painted in the usual khaki and green camouflage. I now completed my driving lessons; for it was possible to turn and back the vehicle over vast areas of concrete, and by now I could reach the pedals. Then, after about eighteen months, the whole project was suddenly abandoned. A huge acreage had been taken over (presumably with compensation to the owners), had then been levelled and covered with concrete, at an enormous cost. Now it was left to the weeds. As far as I know, not a single operational aircraft ever landed there. Millisle was just one of the countless miscalculations of war. Other bases, however, with similar machinery continued to operate, and so my father was transferred to an office in Belfast from which he made periodic tours around the province.

Back in the city, he found a room in a house off Shaftsbury Square, and before long became a member of the Ulster Arts Club nearby in Great Victoria Street. The Club had a bar, a lounge, and a billiards room; and, just as the Clontarf club was not limited to yachtsmen, so the Belfast establishment did not confine itself to aesthetes. Nevertheless, perhaps because of his easy-going nature, my father got on quite well with artists. In Dublin he was a friend of Walter Till, and now he got to know W.H. Conn, whose work appeared regularly in *Dublin Opinion*. In contrast to the paper's other material, Conn's drawings were of nostalgic bitter-sweet subjects, like street scenes in one of Dublin's decaying Georgian squares, or pictures of a rural Ireland that was passing away. One especially striking piece showed an old man sitting on a hillside watching, in reverie, as a group of young people performed a reel. It was called 'The Kerry Dances'. The membership of the Arts Club ranged from academics to shipping magnates, but the man who impressed me most was the huge and celebrated Blair Mayne. I had seen him when he played for Ireland in the late thirties. During the war he earned a fearsome reputation as 'Paddy Mayne' in the Long Range Desert Group, which carried out dangerous and exciting raids behind the enemy's lines. One story described how, when he had run out of grenades, he tore the instrument panel out of a German aircraft with his bare hands. My father told me of a more recent and less glamorous occasion when someone in the club got out of control and started to smash glasses and insult other members. When remonstrance failed, Blair Mayne got to his feet, seized the man by the lapels, and gave him a short, economical, chuck under the chin which knocked him cold. He then carried him gently downstairs and left him in the hallway to sober up. It was said that after the war Blair Mayne found it hard to settle down to a solicitor's life. Certainly when I met him in 1946 his face was that of a man who had supped full of horrors. Not long afterwards he was killed at the wheel of his car. As for my father, it was interesting to see how his new job and new friends altered his view of Ulster. Once, when Billy Conn had gone off to refill our glasses, he said 'You know, these fellows are as good a lot as you'll find anywhere.' There seemed no point in reminding him of his earlier judgments.

Until 1942, or thereabouts, the Headmaster of Methodist College was Mr J.W. Henderson, a large military-looking man with a high public profile. He was always engaged on important business, and when he went down town he wore a bowler hat and sat in the back of a chauffeur-driven saloon. During his tenure he compiled two sumptuous volumes entitled *The Book of MCB* – a history of the school plus a series of potted biographies. For all I know, he may have been a great man. But in a school of 1200 you cannot be a great man and at the same time know what is going on. This second function was assigned to the Vice-Principal, Mr John Falconer. Then, after a decade of rounding up latecomers and putting down smoking in the boys' lavatories, the latter was suddenly elevated to the Headship. Falconer was a small Scotsman with large solemn glasses who made his way round the school at a brisk trot. He once said, in an unguarded moment, that he had thought of becoming a footballer; and indeed it needed little effort to see him bustling about in the box and sending shots streaking past the goalie. As a relic, perhaps, of that earlier ambition, he invariably wore boots. In spite of his new administrative duties 'Johnny the Hawk' continued to teach English and History. He was particularly fond of Shakespeare and Scott, and some of his enthusiasm did come across. Naturally enough, he was most at home with *Macbeth*; and I can still see him girding himself for that final sortie:

'I'll fight, till from my bones my flesh be hack'd./Give me my armour!' He brought the same emotional fervour to *Julius Caesar*. Here one had to accept the initial premise that Mark Antony was a Glaswegian. After that, everything fell into place: 'O, pardon me, thou bleeding piece of airth,/That I am meek and gentle with these bootchers!'

Actually in Falconer's youth Glasgow was no bad place to study Shakespeare. He told us that he and his classmates once had to answer a question on the function of metre. 'And the Professor said that only one essay made any sense.' Then he added with a shy smile, 'That Professor, ye know, was A.C. Bradley.' In fiction his great love was Scott. 'At the moment I'm enjoying the pleasure of deciding which novel I'm going to read in the Easter holidays. I think it may well be *The Fair Maid of Perth*. I suppose I must have read it more than twenty times.' This I found quite amazing. For examinations, I had struggled through *Rob Roy* and *The Talisman*. But to think of reading all that stuff for *pleasure*! He also took us through Thackeray's *Henry Esmond*. In that novel the word 'mistress' occurs quite often, in the courteous deferential sense. Yet the Hawk could never bring himself to pronounce it properly. He always said 'Missus'. Similarly, in *As You Like It*, he always called Jaques 'Jayqueeze'. Granted, the name has two syllables, but we always assumed that the Hawk's exaggerated version was designed to avoid any possible connection with a privy.

One day, after reading one of G.K. Chesterton's Father Brown stories, Mr Falconer concluded, 'There's just one flaw in the solution of this case, you know, and it's this: you cannot get a human body into a postman's bag.' Our next teacher that day was 'Gandhi' Howatson, who was due to explain some of the mysteries of stocks and shares. As he walked into the room his face was that of a gentle seagull; the rest of him was clothed in a coarse and rather battered-looking brownish-grey suit. Laying his books on the desk, he began to write something on the blackboard. As he was doing so, Basil McIvor whispered to me, 'I thought someone said that you couldn't get a human body into a postman's bag.' At that moment Gandhi turned round and caught me with the tears streaming down my face. He acted swiftly, and (oh, the ignominy of it) the head prefect was flung out of the room. Luckily, like his great exemplar, Mr Howatson was an apostle of non-violence. Otherwise I might have suffered serious damage.

Ronnie Marshall, the senior housemaster, was a Yorkshire caterpillar that had gone through the chrysalis of London University and emerged as a cosmopolitan butterfly. One imagined him flitting about the galleries and opera-houses of Europe in the 1930s, wearing a panama hat tilted slightly forward over his blond hair, a fawn pin-stripe suit with a pink shirt, and elegant pointed shoes which he placed one in front of the other as though walking a tight-rope. Those travels were referred to in casual asides which deeply impressed us, e.g., 'At the Hotel Bristol in Vienna that year I happened to be staying in the same corridor as the German General Staff. Every night a row of jack-boots would stand outside their doors, waiting to be polished. And oh how I *longed* to pop a hedgehog into one of General Keitel's!' As he said this, he released an imaginary hedgehog from his long pale fingers – fingers which, with their turned-up ends, seemed ideal for playing Chopin. In fact Ronnie Marshall did have a piano; and several times a week he did try conclusions with Chopin. But sadly his technique was not up to his taste, and when he played the minute waltz it would take an agonizing quarter of an hour. Perhaps predictably, he couldn't pronounce his rs; but instead of offering the usual approximation he would vibrate his lips in the manner of a child imitating a motor car. This idiosyncrasy added something extra to his speech – a speech in which the phrasing was carefully shaped. Thus, when one of the boarders was caught trying to slip into the girls' part of the building, he said, 'This simply pwooves what I had long suspected, that the wetched Baker is as flabby mowally as he is both mentally and physically.' Sometimes the wit had the kind of flavour that one associates with Noel Coward. On a cold day, when the Headmistress of the girls' school (a rather large lady) got up to leave, wearing a heavy fur coat, Ronnie waved a languid arm towards one of his junior staff and murmured, 'There's a dear boy – open the door for Marshall Timoshenko.' In the minutes before Ronnie entered the classroom a number of aspiring Ronnies would already be in action, one elegantly flexing the binding of a book, another brushing back a stray lock of hair, another frantically pressing his fingers on the desk to get the tips to bend upwards, and yet another appealing to the class to 'settle down then *please*'. The most subtle diversion came from Basil McIvor, who with a totally expressionless face could blow through a tiny aperture between his lips, producing a whistle so high as to be only just perceptible. On hearing it, Ronnie would work his jaws from side to side to clear his Eustachian tubes, and finally seize the lobe of one ear and shake it. Yet, when all the giggling had died down, Ronnie Marshall still projected the image of a man of European culture. And that, in wartime Belfast, was no mean achievement.

One morning, before the Senior Grade (now A level) year began, Bos barged into the Latinist S.J. Wilson's room. Wilson was a mild man who (on the principle of *lucus a non lucendo*) was always known as 'Hannibal'. Over the years there must have been many cartoons showing him complete with hat, horn-rim glasses, and attaché-case, sitting on an elephant in an Alpine setting. But it was clear that, for all his meekness, Wilson had devised a technique for dealing with his head of department. 'Excuse me, Mr ... Eh,' said Bos. 'The Ministry has just informed me of the choice of Greek texts for next year's Senior Grade. I have considered the matter and I wish the class to know that the poetic text will be Aeschylus' *Persians*.' 'I see. Hm. I wonder why they offered that. The text is often corrupt.'

'Aye, now boys and girls, Mr Wilson points out that the textual tradition of the *Persians* presents the reader with certain problems.'

'And the choruses are not easy.'

'This is a great dramatic masterpiece, but at times greatness is purchased at a price. In certain passages of the choral odes the lyrical texture is so dense that a simple translation is almost out of reach.'

'What alternative did they suggest, Mr Bullick?'

'Alternative? Ah yes. Let me see. I have the Ministry's letter here.'

Then, putting on his glasses, 'The alternative is a book of Homer.'

'Homer? Quite an opportunity.'

'Boys and girls, Homer is the fountainhead of all European epic. As Matthew Arnold observed, he is eminently rapid and eminently noble.'

'And, if I remember, eminently plain.'

'Aye, eminently plain.'

'He could be within their scope. What book is it?'

'The book is ... *Iliad* 22.'

'That's the death of Hector.'

'This is, in effect, the climax of the poem. Having slain his opponent, Achilles passes leather thongs through the tendons of his heels and then drags the corpse behind his chariot. This, I make bold to say, is the most barbaric act in all literature.'

(When he was under way Bos tended to sound like Macaulay.)

'Well then, I wonder what one should do.'

'Quite. Boys and girls, I have made up my mind; and I am glad to see I have persuaded Mr Wilson. Next year's poetic text will be Homer, *Iliad* Book 22.'

In September a handful of us duly began *Iliad* 22. From time to time the lessons were interrupted. One morning, for instance, the city woke to find the cryptic number 1305 chalked on every lamp-post, starting from Donegall Place and continuing up the Antrim Road. It was obviously a team job; and their chalk had given out somewhere about Cliftonville Road. This caused a stir, because within the school 1305 represented Bos, rather as 666 stood for the Great Beast of the Apocalypse. A certain amount of class time was taken up with fruitless interrogation. No one knew nothin'. Then there was the occasion when, because of some lunch-time business, Bos had brought in a flask and sandwiches. Shortly after class began he said 'Excuse me boys while I just take a ssip of tea.'

He dipped into his briefcase. Then suddenly his expression changed. Slowly he drew out a sodden packet of sandwiches and laid it on the desk. Then came a dripping apple. With some difficulty he salvaged the flask itself, holding it rather gingerly, for the tea was still hot. Finally he turned the brief-case upside down and shook it. A thin stream of amber liquid trickled onto the floor, like the end of a pee. Bos glared around the class. Chuck Evans' hands were broad enough to conceal the lower half of his face. Andy Graham had his head between his fists, concentrating furiously on the text; McIvor as usual preserved control. I was the only one whose shoulders were shaking. In a dangerously low voice Bos snarled. 'I mark your laughter, Rudd. Aye, I mark it. A perfectly good thermos flask smashed to atoms, and all you can do is laugh. There's something seriously wrong with your attitude, Rudd. Your ssystem of values is twisted – aye, twissted.' With that he blinked, shifted his cranium and adjusted the knot of his tie.

Then there was a small matter of style. In translating the *Iliad* Bos liked to finish with a version in the 'antique' manner of Ernest Myers. At the beginning of their final encounter, Achilles says to Hector (according to Myers): 'Bethink thee of all thy soldiership; now behoveth it thee to quit thee as a good spearman and valiant man of war.' Bos improved the first phrase to 'Mind thee of all thy fence.' The rest he simply filched. Then he said 'Niall' (the Christian name was always used in periods of truce) 'will you translate Hector's reply.' I started, 'You will not stick your spear in my back as I run away.' 'What?' roared Bos. 'How *dare* you render the no-bility of Homer in the idiom of the gutter? I sometimes wonder if your prosaic mind, Rudd, has learned *anything* from its exposure to the greatness of Greece', and so on for three minutes. Then, dropping his eyes quickly to Myers, he said, 'Not as I flee shalt thou plant thy spear in my reins …' Forty-five years later, before writing these words, I looked up Richmond Lattimore's version and was amused to find 'You will not stick your spear in my back as I run away from you.' Granted, that does not quite settle the question. Lattimore once told me that in translating the *Iliad* he often felt the lack of an accepted poetic diction, but that, rather than faking grandeur, he had gone for naturalness. So 'you will not stick your spear in my back' may be too low. But as the impro-vised effort of a schoolboy it hardly deserved such fulminations.

In the Senior Grade exam it was my Latin (equably taught by Hannibal) that went awry. Before we took our seats, I glanced once more at Livy's historical sources as enumerated by Butler and Scullard in their edition of Book 30. The paper was handed out, and then my act of folly began. Instead of starting with the pre-pared passages and the questions on the set books, then doing the prose and unseens, and ending with the essay which could be expanded or curtailed, I fastened on the essay topic (Dido and Aeneas) and began to write. Much later, I tackled the prepared pas-sages and the unseens, and then found to my horror that only twenty minutes were left for the prose. Five minutes before the end

I glanced out the window, and to my dismay saw Bos taking up a position near the door, ready to conduct an instant *post mortem*. 'Ah there you are, Niall! I trust you've done well.' 'I'm not sure that I planned my time quite right, sir.' 'Well anyhow let's look at the paper. Hm, nothing wrong with the passages ... the unseens seem do-able ... I take it you gratefully accepted *this*!' 'Which?' 'This old chestnut here "List and write brief notes on Livy's sources", well?' Oh God. 'I'm sorry sir. I ... I must have left that out.' 'Left it *out*?' 'Well, either I didn't notice it, or else I forgot about it.' 'But ... but ... this is sheer ...' 'I'm afraid it is, sir.' Suddenly Bos seemed drained of all his indignation. 'Well well,' he said wearily, 'I doubt you've made a hash of it, Rudd. Aye, a sorry hash of it.' A couple of weeks later, the Chaplain, Eric Gallagher, looked up from his newspaper at breakfast. 'The Senior results are out. Good news for you, Niall. On the arts side you've got second place in the province.' Kind words came from neighbouring chairs, and I duly returned thanks. But inside my head I heard Bos's voice: 'I doubt you've made a hash of it.' And I knew the old sod was right.

Prize-day ceremonies were held, at that time, in the Whitla Hall, which was too small to accommodate parents. But the sight of the girls in white blouses and the staff with their coloured hoods draped over their gowns showed that some kind of official ritual was afoot. There were three elements: the music, the distribution of prizes, and the speeches. For the music, the school orchestra was augmented by any member of staff who could play an instrument. That included Blarge, who in his smartest uniform and with his silken hair combed sideways across his pate officiated at the snare drum. Every year, the girls sang 'Nymphs and shepherds'. Delightful – and very English. Then we would all sing 'Land of hope and glory'. In rehearsals we had been drilled by Dr Stoneley, when we reached the phrase 'who are born of thee', *not* to come in on the beat. Instead, we were to sing '(beat) who-are bo-orn of thee'. But invariably, when we reached that point, a chorus of lusty teenage baritones would come in too soon, singing 'who are bo-orn of thee'. As for the song itself, the *tune* of course was splendid. But even in the 1940s that bit about the empire ever expanding under God's direction was patently absurd. And to hear the words still being bellowed half a century later by those cheerful fatheads at the Proms makes you wonder if England will ever face reality. The last musical item was the school song, which was sung just once every year and which no one ever translated:

> Floreat Ultonia, floreant Hiberni,
> Floreat Collegium nominis aeterni!
> Dumque cum laboribus uitae concertamus,
> Semper in memoria Ludum habeamus.

> (Roughly):
> Long live Ulster and the Irish,
> Long the College and its arts!
> In life's struggles let us ever
> Hold the School within our hearts.

The speeches would begin with the Headmaster's report to the Governors and parents and anyone else who cared to hear. Rehearsing the achievements of the school over the past year, he always did a skilful job. You could recognize the truth of the separate features, but the whole subject had been subtly enhanced and glamorized, like a portrait by a fashionable artist. In reply the frail and kindly Mr Fullerton would congratulate staff and pupils for enabling such a report to be presented. Then, after the prizes had been given out, some local celebrity (an industrial magnate, say, or a Unionist politician, but never a woman) would address the assembly. The usual formula was to congratulate the school once more, to assert that the speaker had never won a prize in his life, to tell a couple of good stories, and to ask for a half holiday. All fair enough. There is nothing wrong with a yearly ceremony of self-congratulation. It asserts the institution's identity, promotes an *esprit de corps* and all that. But to single out the successful, and then load them with valuable objects, does seem rather vulgar. I have the impression that in recent decades more and more schools have abandoned the practice. Maybe they are right.

Meanwhile, the ordinary routine of the boarders' life continued. Every week we would each stuff our dirty clothes into a bag, and then throw the whole lot into a large basket. By now the layout of the laundry used by the College was well known, thanks to a diagram prepared by one of the boys. This diagram showed a square floor with letters running clockwise: A, button-smasher; B, shirt-

tail-ripper; C, sock-shrinker; D, colour-fader, and so on. The joke
was not greatly enjoyed by the authorities, since the laundry was
owned by one of the governors. In the dormitories we had individual cubicles – a great advance on the 'public ward' design which
prevailed at many schools. When the master on duty came to put
out the lights, he would find one boy doing a handstand, another
practising a swing quarter turn as taught by Victor Sylvester,
another putting his army trousers under the mattress or wrapping
his damp rugby togs round the pipe that ran along the skirting.
Someone else, with a crimson face, would be blowing into a length
of brass tubing which was supposed to prevent him from falling out
of the window. Someone else again would be hanging from an
overhead bar until his arm-muscles squeaked. (Records were estab-
lished even for such pointless masochism as that.) When the lights
were out we would settle down with our head-phones; for everyone
had either a crystal set of his own or else a lead from somebody
else. Geraldo and Dorothy Carless, Billy Ternant, Joe Loss, and
the rest seemed like old friends. That was also the period when
cinema organs were played by Reginald Dixon, Reginald Foort, and
Reginald Porter-Brown; in fact, some years earlier, I had asked my
father what you had to do to become a Reginald. In the morning
the first (electric) bell went off at 7.15 for those who wanted to
shave, shower, dress, and walk calmly to the dining hall for breakfast at 8. They were not a large company. A quarter of an hour later
came the voice of Ronnie Marshall on the way to his bath. 'Come
along then, please. It's going on for eight.' 'But sir, it's only 7.32.'
'Quite. If it's after half-past seven it's going on for eight! Tee-hee-
hee.' The second bell went at 7.45. Still time for a quick shower. By
five to eight conversation would cease, as people concentrated on
finding their clothes and doing the minimum of acrobatics to get
into them (vest, shirt and pullover would usually go on together).
As the hand-bell rang, there was a rush for the door. Jackets could
be put on as the boys sped down the stairs, hair was smoothed and
ties straightened in the final sprint along the corridor.

From 1940 on, several masters left to join up. Mr Vernon Gay, a
physical-education specialist trained at Loughborough, joined the
RAF. As a temporary replacement the school engaged an ex-army
PT sergeant called Tony Miles. Miles was a short, dark Dubliner

whose camel-hair overcoat and fancy hairstyle gave him the appearance of a 'spiv' or a 'wide boy', and who walked with a bit of a swagger. He won immediate respect by showing he could do everything he asked *us* to do – but far better. His agility on horse, bar and mat was amazing, and he could shin up a twenty-foot rope in the sitting position. He also taught us the rudiments of boxing. Here he had the unpleasant habit of using me as a sparring-partner. 'Today we are goin' to practise de left hook. Judd, for purposes of demonstration step farword.' These sessions did not lead to anything. In my first two years I had boxed in the annual championships, largely because the High School in Dublin had encouraged the sport and old Frosty Nelson's son Johnny (another ex-sergeant) had been a good instructor. But I didn't much like the atmosphere of the tournament, and by the age of fourteen I had realized that boxing was a mug's game. At the same time, perhaps because John Falconer was inclined towards pacifism, the sport faded out and was never missed. In the summer Tony Miles coached athletics, in which his favourite event was the pole-vault. Somehow he procured a long bamboo pole, had a wooden box sunk in front of the high-jump, and persuaded a handful of us to have a go. It was good enough fun, but no one got much above nine feet. Even that could be uncomfortable, for in those days there was no pile of foam rubber to land on. You just hit the sand and hoped for the best. In other events he found more talent, and he helped one boy to set new Ulster records in shot and discus. There was a sad side to it all, however. For while 'Strucky Miles' got on splendidly with the boys (who were indifferent to matters of class), he never fitted into the staff common room. Outside the school he seemed to have few cronies; and he lived a rather lonely life in the basement of a house in College Gardens. I wonder what he was paid.

In our scholarship year someone, apparently, decided that we could do with 'broadening'. So we were told to attend a weekly class in Civics, which would be given by a Mr McElroy. We never quite found out what he was. He showed up every week wearing battledress, and there were rumours that he had some connection with the Department of Education in Queen's University. I'm not sure that the Methodist College authorities quite realized what

they'd got. On the first day he said, 'You know the only way forward for this country lies in the nationalization of the means of
production, distribution, and exchange.' It was the first time I had
heard that famous formula, but in the next few weeks Mr McElroy
proceeded to fill in a blueprint for a socialist utopia. In a society
whose motto was 'From each according to his ability to each
according to his need' the old satanic mills would be demolished,
new factories would spring up, owned and run by 'the people', and
producing goods for 'the people'. This entity called 'the people'
would no longer live in city centres but in newly designed satellite
towns, where adequate 'housing' (never 'houses') would be provided. In other contexts 'society' tended to take the place of the people. Thus 'society' would see to it that 'the pre-school age-group'
received 'proper nourishment'; 'society' would not permit a strati-
fied and discriminatory system of education; the past would be
studied as a series of imperfect stages (slave-owning societies, feu-
dalism, capitalism) leading up to the present; art would be relevant
to the needs of 'society', and so on. Most of us could see that his
vision was inspired by a genuine idealism. (And of course in the
post-war years Mr Attlee's government, fuelled by the spirit of wartime unity, would take the country some distance down that road.)
Yet, as presented by Mr McElroy, it all sounded rather abstract.
'Society' seemed like something uniform and anonymous, and 'the
people' did not sound the same as 'people'. Perhaps these reserva-
tions were unfair, for in itself idealism is more appealing than officially sanctified greed. Nevertheless, some members of the class
lost interest. One day, five minutes before we were due to begin,
Chuck Evans passed by the window, heading for the Eglantine Inn
on Malone Road. 'Brothers', he said, with a very passable imitation
of McElroy's Scots accent, 'while you are listening to McElroy in
that piece of substandard housing, I am going to join some reac-
tionary elements for a bit of liquid nourishment and a game of bul-
liards.' As we hurled recriminations after him, he turned round, and
with a maddening wave called, 'Keep the red flag flying!'

In the first six months of 1946 life took many forms, including
cadet force parades, rugby matches, rehearsals for *Agamemnon*, and
outings with a girl I had met at a party the previous November (a
heady experience, this, rather like one's first liqueur). But none of

these things had anything to do with the central reason for being at school, which was to prepare for Sizarship (i.e. the entrance scholarship examination to Trinity College, Dublin). One of my teachers was James Harrison, who had just come out of the RAF. His unit had co-operated closely with the Americans, with the result that his Ulster accent had acquired a definite transatlantic twang. He had taken a first at TCD just before the war, and he now settled down to a career in teaching, during which he produced some clear and elegant text-books. The other teacher (also a TCD first) was Drew Donaldson, an intriguingly complex man. He had rebelled against the religious ethos of his home, and would sometimes joke about his mother's habit of referring to Mrs X as 'a firm Protestant' and Mrs Y as 'a bigoted Catholic'. Again, although he had chosen to teach Classics, he was a first-rate engineer. In his house on the Lisburn Road he had installed a model railway, replicating a section of the Great Southern system, and this could be operated in exact accordance with the company's peacetime schedule. In addition, he had made all the locomotives and rolling stock himself, with an obsessive accuracy. He had even obtained the right paint from the railway-yard to ensure authenticity. The Railway, in its turn, was so impressed with his work that it regularly asked him to lend his models for exhibition. This cast of mind was reflected in his teaching of early Roman history, for which he prepared charts like super railway-timetables, illustrating Rome's relations with her various neighbours in different coloured inks. He had almost no interest in literature, but was fascinated by the structure of Greek and Latin. Not surprisingly, he had done very well at comparative philology. One could imagine him eagerly absorbing all those dreadful Indo-European paradigms (Sanskrit, Greek, Latin, Old High German, Irish etc. etc.) and mastering at a glance the laws of Grimm, Verner, and Grassmann. Today, no doubt, he would go in for Linguistics, or perhaps become a computer man. One result of his interest in language (a result which, in view of the traditional approach to Greek and Latin, was less bizarre than it sounds) was a considerable dexterity in composing Greek and Latin verses. As an elementary competence in this was required for my exam, I used to see him regularly for correction and advice. One evening, early on, I

knocked on his door and asked if he was feeling lyrical. He immediately accepted this ironical fiction, which implied that he was
unable to put iam-bics and elegiacs together except in the white
heat of inspiration. He, in turn, promoted another fiction, which
he claimed to have learned from Freud, namely that the human
memory could not seize hold of anything except through some
form of sexual association. So, when leaving a note to remind him
of a tutorial later that evening, I would try to place the piece of
paper in a suitable setting, for example behind two ink-bottles and
a vertical ruler.

Drew's interest in Irish was another aspect of his rebellion
against his Protestant Ulster background. The more he studied the
language, the more he felt himself drawn to pre-plantation Ireland. In the end, one summer, he put his bike on the train, and
went off to live in the Gaeltacht. After several visits he became
quite fluent. He also became more nationalist in his politics,
though (as far as I know) he never seriously thought of joining the
IRA. Back in school, as a public declaration of his loyalties, he
began to use green ink – a habit which made him highly unpopular
at the end of the first term. For, on receiving a batch of about
thirty reports, each of which had already been annotated by six or
eight of his colleagues, Drew added his marks and comments in
green. This defiant gesture so annoyed the Head that he ordered
all the reports to be destroyed and re-written, insisting that Drew
should use ink of an acceptable blue or black. To work off his various frustrations, Drew used to jump on his bicycle and ride long
distances at a furious speed. This habit eventually brought on a
heart attack, which resulted in his premature death. When I heard
the news, I thought of our joint composing sessions. One piece
which we did was a Latin version of the song beginning

> She is far from the land where her young hero sleeps,
> And lovers around her are sighing,
> But coldly she turns from their gaze and weeps,
> For her heart in his grave is lying.

Subject and setting were just right for elegiacs; unfortunately
our version was mediocre, and even contained a false quantity. In
spite of these defects it appeared in the school magazine. In retro-

spect its publication was clearly one of Drew's sly jokes. He had used the Latin form as a disguise to smuggle a nationalist song into an Ulster Protestant magazine. For the girl is Sarah Curran; and her dead lover is the executed patriot, Robert Emmet.

As I indicated at the start of this chapter, wartime conditions at Methodist College were dreary – the black-out, the poor food, the impossibility of travel, the shortage of staff, and so on. But these privations were far less than those suffered by many children in England, and quite trivial when compared to the disasters taking place on the Continent. The teaching on the whole was good, and while there were occasional high spirits in the classroom, there was never any problem of discipline. As far as I was concerned, the school rescued me from a disintegrating home; it provided education, sport, a few close friends, and even a touch of romance. In my last two years there, I lived with an intensity, and with a kind of elation that I never knew again. And (a thing which I could never have foreseen) I was sadder at leaving than I was when I arrived.

Ballymoney

From the selfish viewpoint of a visitor, the war did Ballymoney a service, for it granted a seven-year reprieve from the blight of twentieth-century development. As there was virtually no petrol for private use, cars disappeared from the roads. In Dublin, for a while, gas was used as a substitute, and on a windy day there was usually at least one gas-bag to be seen which had torn loose from the roof of its car and was now floating down O'Connell Street at a height of thirty feet. But soon bags, too, disappeared and older travellers reverted to the train. Not that there was anything like a peacetime schedule. Turf was no substitute for coal, and there were times when the crew had to 'bail out', i.e. clean out the loco-motive's fire and re-light it with timber gathered along the route. It is on record that a train travelling from Dublin to Athlone was passed twice by a canal barge when engaged upon this operation.' People bound for Ballymoney would board the train at Harcourt Street station and, eventually, alight at Gorey. They would travel the rest of the way by pony and trap. Youngsters relied on bicycles. At thirteen I was allowed to have a full-size machine; so I chose an exciting BSA sports model with black handlebars and a Sturmey-Archer three-speed hub. Price £8. When I went back to school, Mrs Daly (mother of Miss Dorrie and Miss Edie), who was now well on in her seventies, told me I could leave it in her house. So I carried it up to a third-floor attic, turned it upside down on a sheet of newspaper, let some air out of the tyres, and then, without thin-king, snapped on a heavy padlock and chain. 'That ought to make sure that no one steals it,' said Mrs Daly. In the summer of 1941 my cousin Joan and I rode to Ballymoney for the first time. It was over sixty miles from Clontarf, and we weren't used to the exercise; so we stopped more and more frequently as time went on. At one point, just north of Arklow, we lay exhausted in the middle of the road with our bikes sprawled beside us. Anyone doing that now would be dead within a minute. (The bike survived one more ordeal. In Belfast I was returning to school through the black-out with a friend on the cross-bar. As we were in a hurry, I decided to take a short cut across a bombsite. Predictably, we crashed. When we picked ourselves up, we found that the vertical stem which held the handlebars in place was bent almost ninety degrees. So we had to run the rest of the way. Afterwards I cut off the bent bit with a hacksaw and jammed the stump down into the socket. It rusted into place, and the machine was still ridable when, ten years on, I sold it to a vicar in Hull.)

In the 1940s, then, Ballymoney in neutral Ireland relapsed into quietness. By day this was disturbed on occasion by Peter Dawson singing 'Drake's Drum' or 'Devon, Glorious Devon', or by that incomparable bass Malcolm MacEachern (Mr Jetsam) singing 'The Windmill', or by Vera Lynn's rendering of 'A Nightingale Sang in Berkeley Square'. This last record was a green-label 78 with the unpleasant 'A Little King without a Crown' on the other side. Vera Lynn's other hits were familiar through my school crystal-set – 'Yours', 'We'll Meet Again', 'The White Cliffs of Dover' and (the only song popular on both sides during the war) 'Lili Marlene'. Her rather harsh voice with its intermittent sobs was less admired by older relatives. My Uncle Ernest once asked, 'Who *is* that caterwauling woman?'

At night other sounds reminded us uneasily of war; for sometimes one could hear the faint hum of aircraft flying up the Irish Sea. It was said that Luftwaffe pilots would check their position from the lights of Dublin and then turn east to Liverpool and other midland cities. In 1940 there were also rumours that the Germans intended to invade Ireland to effect a back-door entry into England. We would be reminded of these rumours when Big Jack Leary passed the Bungalow's gate at dusk with a shotgun at the trail. 'I'm off on pathrawl', he would say. After the war, it came to light that the Germans had indeed prepared plans for Operation Green, whereby nearly four thousand troops would land in

S.E. Ireland and establish a bridgehead from Gorey, through Thomastown and Clonmel, down to Dungarvan.[10] It is not known how serious these plans were meant to be. Even if the landing, however, had been no more than a diversion, it would still have been catastrophic. And we were all old enough by now to realize that an airborne division of Germans was not going to be halted by the sight of Big Jack with a shotgun. Rabbits, in fact, were a more likely explanation of his patrols. The war was brought home to us more directly by the departure of both Jack Rickerby, who served on the highly dangerous motor torpedo-boats, and his brother Len, who at one stage was a cook on the old battleship *Repulse*. (Len, who had retained the cockney speech of his very early days, once amazed us by saying, 'My mites calls me Paddy because of my Irish accent.') My cousin, Buddy Polden, whose home I then shared, joined the navy. He served as an able seaman in a destroyer on the Arctic convoy route, and subsequently commanded a tank landing-craft in the Mediterranean. His friend, Billy Sterling, another regular guest at the Bungalow, joined the army and survived the horrors of Anzio and Monte Cassino.

For two or three weeks every summer we were joined in the Bungalow by Uncle Ernest, i.e. Dr W.E. Cooke, who in about 1910 had given up his job in a Dublin bank and, some years later, qualified as a doctor. Specializing in tropical medicine, he had travelled to Malaya in the 1920s, and had kept a diary of his meetings with colleagues and their opinions about various forms of treatment. The diary is now in the London Hospital for Tropical Diseases, where he was on the staff for many years. He also had a room in the Harley Street Clinic, where he saw people who worked in Africa, India and (before the war) the Far East. He did a lot for the missionary societies and also worked at a centre outside London for the treatment of leprosy. So on any objective assessment he was quite a distinguished man, who did a disproportionate amount of good. But 'a prophet is not without honour', and in the family circle he was treated with a sort of affectionate ridicule. While a reasonable amount of decorum was preserved in his presence, our antennae were always on the alert for characteristic anecdotes and phrases. A fairly typical narrative would have gone something like this: 'Yesterday I was just leaving the rooms to catch the boat-train, when Mary showed in the most *enormous* man. Not much over six foot, perhaps, but 'pon my soul the fellow was almost *spherical*. At the end of the examination I put him on the scales, and there it was – 18$\frac{1}{2}$ stone. I said to him, "Well sir, it wouldn't do any harm to lose a bit of weight." "I can't, docthor, I'm a chef.'" (For some reason his punch lines were usually delivered in a fake bog-Irish accent.) There would then have followed an account of the hectic rush to Euston and of how he had *just* caught the train. At such points one had the picture of a smallish, thickset figure with grey hair, a navy blue suit, and an Old Wesley tie, diving to seize hold of the buffers as the train began to pull out. Then, continuing, 'As luck would have it, the brother sitting opposite began to smoke a most pesti*len*tial pipe. So I had to point to the notice on the window, "I'm afraid, sir, this is a non-smoker." With very poor grace he took himself and his noisome shag next door. Then finally, when we reached Holyhead, I noticed someone else had left a pair of drumsticks on his seat. So as we walked off the platform I came up behind the man and tapped him on the shoulder with the drumsticks. You could hardly credit it, but he turned round and swung his fist at my face! Had it not been for the old rugby training, I declare I'd have measured my length on the ground. I said, "You, sir, are a most un*manner*ly fellow!" That's the sort you get travelling these days. The Lord was good. Otherwise I would have ended with a fractured jaw. And all because of a pair of dhrum-sticks!'

In his lodgings in Norbury, where he was cared for with great kindness for thirty years, he was a sort of permanent PG. The others, mostly students, would come and go in two- or three-year cycles. This meant, fortunately, that the audience for his stories was regularly renewed. A typical tale concerned the lady in the music-hall who felt she ought to recognize the tune being played by the orchestra. She said to the man beside her, 'Go and look at that notice over there and see what they're playing.' When he returned she said, 'Well, did you find out what it is?' 'I did, ma'am,' he said, "it's the refrain from shpittin".' The last time I visited him in Norbury (this was in the late 1950s), we left together for town. As soon as we were out of the gate, he broke into a gentle jog-trot, carrying as always a small brown attaché-case. As the fastenings had long since broken, the case was secured by a strap. Once, when the handle too had come undone, it was mended temporarily with the stump of a banana. Alighting from the bus, we jogged to the train, jogged to the underground, shouldered aside some people on the escalator, 'Stand right, walk left, please', changed at Charing Cross, still jogging, and finally emerged at Regent's Park for the final sprint to Harley Street. He was then seventy-eight.

In his youth he had been a good tennis-player. (One story described the fiendish cunning with which he had defeated the favourite, Van Allen, in the finals at Eastbourne in 1904.) He seems to have taken the game seriously – so seriously, in fact, that according to Uncle Herbert he used to make his tennis matches a subject of prayer. 'It was bad enough to play *him*, but to have to play him *and* the Almighty was really a bit unfair.' Uncle Ernest was also a keen rugby follower and regularly watched a game on Saturdays. While he supported London Irish, he was well enough disposed to all the London clubs, except the Harlequins, presumably because they were the headquarters club and rather too successful. As he was inclined to conspiracy-theories, he took the view that several of the London referees were pro-Harlequin. It has to be admitted that some of his dislikes amounted to prejudice – nothing virulent, but still clearly perceptible. He was not only anti-smoking and anti-alcohol, but also anti-Semitic, anti-black, and anti-Catholic. He always referred to Catholics as *Roman*-Catholics, by which he implied that while all Christians were Catholic, the *Roman*-Catholics represented a kind of early splinter group. It would not be possible to include all his antipathies in a single illustration. But you would be making a good start if you could picture someone like, say, the late Sammy Davis Jr, under the influence of drink, smoking a pipe, and wearing a Harlequins jersey. In the main, these dislikes were general, and were almost invariably over-ridden by personal acquaintance; but in one or two cases his antipathies were quite specific, as with 'Misther Áneurin Beván, who has wished this infernal health-service on us'. I never knew whether his mispronunciation of Bevan's name was deliberate (to distinguish him from Mr Ernest Bevin) or unconscious; but I recalled that his father, old James H. Cooke, would always refer to the Irish prime minister as 'Mr de Valéra'.

In his long career in London he naturally came to know some quite eminent people in the medical world, like Sir John Weir (the Queen's physician) and Sir Archie McIndoe, the plastic surgeon; and I was interested, during one visit, to hear Sir Philip Manson-Bahr (an authority on tropical medicine) address him affectionately as 'Cookie'. When he introduced a member of his own family to any of these people, he would add some detail to build us up and prevent us from feeling over-awed. This could be acutely embarrassing. Once, just after I had got my first job as an assistant lecturer, Uncle Ernest introduced me to the Rev. Donald Soper, adding 'this young man is a *classical* scholar'. Soper smiled and said 'Ah, so we'll have to be careful when quoting the text of the Greek Testament!' Something rather similar happened to a friend and relative, Bobby Mitchell, who ran a long-established wine business in Dublin. At dinner in a London hotel, when a very dignified wine-waiter advanced with the wine-list, Uncle Ernest said, 'You had better know that my guest is a *connoisseur*,' which seemed to imply 'just in case you were thinking of steaming off the labels'. He then added, 'He knows more about wine than you ever will.'

As he approached eighty, Uncle Ernest would sometimes talk of retiring – of coming back to Ireland and perhaps giving the odd consultation. On hearing this report for the third time, Uncle Stan said, 'Consultation? On tropical diseases? Why, he wouldn't find a *cat* with sprue over here.' In the event he never did return to Ireland, but he regularly spent his summer holidays in Ballymoney. Sometimes, indeed, he *was* asked for his medical opinion; and then his usual recommendation was 'Try Iodex'. This was the counterpart of Uncle Willie's 'Drink plenty of water'. The two of them reminded me of that GP in Shaw's *The Doctor's Dilemma* who, whatever the complaint, would always prescribe 'a pound of ripe greengages'. In the Bungalow he was frequently told off by his sister. 'Really Ernest, those old golf-trousers ought to be *burnt*!' 'It's *much* too cold for bathing today; you'll give yourself a heart attack!' 'How late did you sit up with that book? It's no *wonder* you spend half the day asleep!' 'Don't *tell* me you're off to that river again. I don't believe there's a single trout *in* it.' Uncle Ernest accepted this nagging with wry resignation, and continued as before. He did not give up sea-bathing, though he took with him a

hypodermic with adrenalin, wrapped in a towel. (Who was supposed to administer it?) His late-night reading included an old
green paperback detective story called *The Drowsy Mosquito*, which
he read anew every summer, having forgotten the plot in the intervening period. And he would still cycle off to a nearby river.
(Once, returning late for supper, he gave an account of his expedition, not realizing that two of his great-nephews had set up a tape
recorder. The tape ends, characteristically, '... and bad scran to it,
I fell in a ditch and got thoroughly wet'.) Having absorbed, as it
were, his sisters' attacks, he then went over to the offensive. To a
chorus of protest, he would tell medical stories at the dinner-table.
One, for example, concluded, '... you can imagine how dear old
Muggleton's face changed when he opened the box of chocolates.
He had assumed it was another batch of stools for analysis.'
'Really, Ernest. *Please!*' 'Better than the other way round, what?'
Once, with the insouciance of a long-established bachelor, he
removed his false teeth, licked the plate, and then scraped it
absent-mindedly on his lapel. And then, the final outrage, one
morning he took up the chamberpot, which he had been given as a
special privilege to save an eighty-year-old from having to walk to
the loo, and emptied the contents onto a clump of mint that was
growing under his window. For that, he was almost sent back to
Norbury.

I don't suppose the weather at Ballymoney had a wider range
than anywhere else, but we were more aware of it as we were usually out of doors. At Easter there were often chilly days with a
brisk wind blowing from Tara Hill; the clear light made the gorse
and primroses stand out all the more sharply against their green
background; and every now and then one caught a whiff of smoke
from a turf fire. In the summer there would be a few days of bright
windless calm, when the sea was unusually far out and the surf was
the faintest ripple. From a boat you could see shoals of jellyfish
floating along in the clear, lime-coloured water; and there were
bass lazing round, just off Old Man Rock. That was good camping
weather, too. One year, when I was about nine, a small grubby tent
appeared on the grassy headland opposite the gate. After a while I
went over to investigate, and found the owners were away. Peering
through the flap, I saw that almost the whole space was filled by a

large white piano-accordion and an equally large glass frame. The frame contained a prayer in ornamental writing which said 'God bless our home'. Later, I asked one of the men what he played on his accordion. He said something that sounded like 'Nuthra's Knickers'. I was too polite to ask him to repeat it, and no one at the Bungalow was able to solve the puzzle.

On stormy days no camping was possible; one sometimes saw people huddled miserably behind a hedge after their tent had blown away. If the storm brought prolonged rain, the river came roaring down the valley and barely managed to squeeze under the stone bridge. Then it would hurl itself down to the beach in great white and amber cascades, and rush across the sand to meet the incoming surf. Out at sea long lines of creamy breakers advanced towards the land, gathering themselves up for the last wild plunge that would send them sizzling up the beach. In weather like that one thought of the terrible December night in 1947 when the engine of the old schooner *Isaalt* (*sic*) failed, and she was wrecked on the rocks less than half a mile up the coast. One of the crew managed to climb the cliffs in the dark and raise the alarm, but it was too late. On the next day two bodies were washed ashore, but those of Captain McGuinness and a lady passenger were never found. Slowly over the years the wreck broke up. Now there is nothing left but the fly-wheel. In the main, that stretch of coast is safe for sailing, and for bathing. But once, when we were at lunch, a man came running up to the bridge shouting for help; a girl was drowning on the north beach. Everyone hurried around the headland, but by then she had disappeared. Fifteen minutes later, after much fruitless diving, it was decided that the shore-fishing net should be used to bring in her body. The net was paid out in a semi-circle and drawn ashore in a horrified silence; and when the last section came in, there was the girl in her blue costume and white bathing-cap lying limply in the meshes. Desperate efforts were made to revive her, but after half an hour a doctor pronounced her dead.

At the end of the war my cousin, Tony Polden (son of Uncle Herbert), and I bought an eight-foot sailing dinghy from Bobby Mitchell for a nominal sum. First we got a sheet of metal from the forge in Gorey to act as a centre-board. Then, after caulking the gaps in the timbers, we glued a layer of thick canvas over the hull and painted the whole lot green. It was just light enough for the two of us to lift it down to the water's edge. One would sit ready at the oars while the other held the stern. Then, in the lull between waves, the latter would push off and fall in a heap onto the stern seat, while the oarsman pulled frantically to avoid the next breaker. Once a week, if it wasn't too rough, we would leave the sailing gear behind and row out to one of the trawlers that used to operate half a mile or so off shore. We would pass up a large bucket, and the crew would fill it with dabs and plaice for about two shillings. Sometimes, if we knew the men, we would clamber on board and spend an hour lazing around and chatting, while the trawler thumped its way up the Wexford coast. Then, after the net had been pulled in, the boat would turn and come down again. Allowing for the tide (flood north, ebb south), we would cast off and row back to Ballymoney. On the Saint Mary, the trawler we knew best, Big Jack Leary was one of the crew. Once, on a hot August afternoon as I lay dozing on the deck, dressed only in a pair of shorts, Big Jack turned to Tony with a grin: 'Let's play a joke on Niles.' He then drew up a bucket of seawater, crept up behind me, and threw the whole lot over his naked passenger. This subtle jest was greeted with Homeric laughter by the rest.

One morning it was so calm and clear that we could see the three-mile buoy on the horizon. We were already quite far off shore when one of us said, 'What about going out to it?' The other agreed, and an hour or so later there we were, holding onto the rusty red surface of the twelve-foot-high buoy, and trying to recover our strength. Before heading back, some kind of triumphant gesture seemed to be called for; so each in turn stood up and peed ceremoniously on the object which symbolized official limits. After that act of hubris we started on the long journey back and landed exhausted nearly two hours later. Then we had to face our mothers.

On another day, when the wind was blowing from the northeast and a few white clouds were moving across the sky, Tony and I sailed out about half a mile and then reached south towards the Courtown Strand. Halfway along the beach, which was quite deserted, we went ashore and hauled the dinghy up the white sand.

After stowing the gear, we took out the rowlocks, and then wandered across a line of dunes into the woods of the Courtown demesne. As we made our way along a path parallel to the beach, the sky was occasionally visible above the treetops, and the sun poured through the gaps forming pools of light on the ground. Suddenly, through a clearing, slightly inland, we saw a small timber house. It had a steeply pitched roof, and casement windows with diamond-shaped panes. We stepped onto the porch and found the front door open. The house was quite empty and was beginning to show signs of neglect – a floorboard gone here, a door half off its hinges there, and a few panes missing from the windows. 'This must be Lady Charlotte's cottage,' said Tony. 'What a place!' I had heard the name before, but knew nothing of the lady, except that she had been a member of the Courtown family. As I moved over to a corner, where the sun was slanting through the glass, I noticed some writing on one of the shutters. Oh no. How could anyone scrawl graffiti in such a room? But, as I looked more closely, it turned out to be this, beautifully written in black ink:

> There is a pleasure in the pathless woods,
> There is a rapture on the lonely shore,
> There is society, where none intrudes,
> By the deep Sea, and music in its roar.
> Byron, *Childe Harold's Pilgrimage*

So somebody else had stood there (how many years ago?) and found the right words.

Once every summer, the younger members of the connection would cycle inland about fifteen miles to Ballydaniel, near the village of Camolin. This was a farm of 130 acres, owned by Mr Richard Graham (locally 'Gram'), who was married to Aunt Annie (a Cooke). Aunt Annie's unmarried sister, Aunt Maggie, also lived there. When you turned in the gate, there was a tall monkey-puzzle tree on your right. The house stood about twenty-five yards from the road. It was a middle-size, unpretentious, farmhouse built (at a rough guess) about 1850 – solid and comfortable, but without modern amenities. Old Richard Graham saw no need for such things, and the women, presumably, had been unable to persuade him. So although there may have been an outside WC, there was certainly no electricity. The most interesting thing in the house was the open fireplace in the kitchen, where a glowing heap of turf and logs could be blown into a blaze by some sort of fan underneath the hearth. The fan was operated by a large wheel, which Nellie, an elderly maid, would allow us to whirl round. The floor was of stone flags; there was an iron spit above the fireplace, and overhead, in the rafters, there were hooks for curing flitches of bacon. Off the kitchen was the dairy, cool and shady, with pans of milk, and a big churn for making butter. Out behind was the yard, with the usual farm buildings.

On one of our visits Aunt Maggie said, 'Come on now and I'll show you how to milk a cow.' She took up a pail and walked out to the milking-shed, carrying her head, with its patrician nose, at a slightly prim angle. (Someone once observed that Aunt Maggie often looked as if she had detected a faintly disagreeable smell.) 'Now you put your stool here, and settle down. Then you place the pail between your knees, tilting it slightly forward, like this. You take hold of one of her udders, and then you squeeze and pull down at the same time.' And with that a thin jet of milk spurted out, hitting the bottom of the pail with a loud tinny sound. 'Now it's your turn. Suzie's a very quiet lady; and anyhow, sure there's nothing to it.' So I sat down, and after some inexpert wrenching, which produced no result, I gradually began to get the hang of it. Things were going quite well, when suddenly I pressed my knees together too hard and the pail shot out, clattering onto the cobble-stones beneath the startled cow. Instinctively Suzie lashed out, and before I knew it I'd been sent sprawling a couple of yards across the cowshed. Picking myself up and checking for damage, I found that her hoof had ripped my trousers and left a painful graze, about five inches long, down the inside of my left thigh. At this point I heard a sort of strangled gurgle and looked up to see Aunt Maggie leaning against the wall helpless with laughter. Back inside the house, Aunt Annie lent me a pair of Richard Graham's trousers while repairs were carried out on mine. The sensation was like walking round inside a furze-bush. When, finally, I put my own pair back on and rejoined the company in the sitting-room, people were still showing the effects of amusement. 'Wasn't it a good thing, now, she didn't aim an inch higher!' said Aunt Maggie, and there was a fresh gust of hilarity.

Five miles from Ballymoney, the main Dublin to Wexford road climbs up through Gorey, with its wide main street. In the 30s and 40s at the bottom of the hill, off to the left, was the garage run by Harry and Percy Bates. Although motoring languished during the war, another branch of their business enjoyed a steady and reliable demand, for they were the local undertakers. One evening Percy put down his glass and said, 'Ah well, I have to go back now and knock something together for poor Mrs O'Sullivan, God rest her.' Someone whose inhibitions had been lowered by drink said, 'But how do you know what size to make the coffin?' 'Ah sure I've known her for years. And if there's anyone I *don't* know, I just slip into the room and throw me eye over them. Of course you have to make a decent job of it. Now when I've made the box, before I put in the lining, I give all the joints a lick of pitch. And then I give it all a nice coat of varnish.' '*Pitch?*' 'Surely. *All* my coffins get a lick of pitch and, I warrant ye, divil the one o' them has laked yit.' As you went up the street you passed Mr Davis's lamp-shop on your left. In those days electricity was by no means universal, and for those who still burned paraffin Mr Davis (or Aladdin as we called him) offered a range of lamps in many shapes and sizes, some with ornamental brass-work and pink tinted globes – the sort of thing that now ranks as an antique and is priced accordingly. Then came the newsagent and local historian Tom Leggatt, known to us as 'The Papal Legate', though as far as I am aware he had no leanings towards Rome. Farther on was Mr Herbert Cooke's Arcade with its glass awning reaching out over the pavement. Inside, a balcony ran round the shop which was lit by a skylight in the roof. It sold all kinds of clothing. Beyond that was Redmond the butcher; his beef was as fine as any I've ever tasted. And so on up the hill to the Church of Ireland, whose site represented a long-vanished social dominance.

Apart from its tarred surface, the main street itself, with its carts drawn by horses or donkeys and its sporadic piles of dung, looked as it had looked for over a century. There were no cars or lorries, no bus-loads of tourists *en route* to Dublin. It was as if, in those six years of war, the grey old town was asserting its historic

Irish character for the last time, before succumbing to an undifferentiated progress. Halfway up on the right was a white building – Cooke's Medical Hall – which was run by Mr Jim Cooke. Here progress had already started. True, one window contained a pair of very tall glass flasks with thin graceful necks, one full of red, and the other a deep blue liquid; inside the shop there was still a shelf with jars containing strange substances, and beneath that a set of drawers with intriguing labels (Mag. Sulph., Nux. Vom., Acetyl. Salicyl.), all of which went back to the days when the chemist made up individual prescriptions. But as well as that, there was now a range of patent medicines. Another counter was given over to cosmetics; yet another to photography. We, however, were primarily interested in the soda fountain, which dispensed excellent milk shakes and ice-cream sodas. (Thanks to the availability of cream and of beet sugar, Irish ice-cream never sank to the level of the stuff produced in Britain.)

The Medical Hall was also the centre of some kind of dental practice. I was never clear about this, because Jim Cooke was not a qualified dentist. The extent of his operations may perhaps be seen in the saying which I often heard: 'No one can pull a tooth like Mr Cooke.' Another question that was once raised had to do with his line in perfumes. 'I sometimes wonder where Jim gets his scent these days,' said Aunt Connie. 'Who knows?' said my mother, 'perhaps he makes it himself.' There was a brief pause, in which one of them must have suppressed a snigger. 'Really, dear! I sometimes think you have a very low mind!' '*Me*? I like *that*!' When Jim Cooke (who was yet another Uncle) died, I drove Aunt Kathleen, Uncle Willie and Uncle Stan down to the funeral service, which took place in the Church of Ireland. It was a sad occasion, for everyone had pleasant memories of him; and some of the memories reached back well into the nineteenth century. As we filed into the pew, I was beside Aunt Kathleen, who looked austerely splendid in her black outfit – an effect enhanced by the presence of a monocle in her right eye. We listened to those grand and moving words from I Corinthians 15 that have brought comfort to Christians for two millennia. Then we knelt down, and suddenly, as the Vicar prayed, there was a little tinkling sound, and Aunt Kathleen began to lean this way and that, making sweeping motions with her hands. Then came a whisper 'Can you help? I've dropped my confounded glass.' Such incidents, of course, don't *always* happen; but when they do, they remind us that the eternal and the ephemeral do not cancel each other out, or even detract from one another. They simply coexist in different dimensions.

When the Bungalow lot went to church in Gorey, they would go to the Methodist church. Here Aladdin took up the collection. He wore patent-leather boots and a neat suit, and his white moustache was always carefully waxed and then twirled into points. He would present the plate to each pew with a ceremonious bow, and then carry it up to the front with impressive dignity. More often, however, they would go to the Church of Ireland at Kiltennel on the Courtown estate. In summer the church was well filled. But if one mentally subtracted the visitors, including a company of the Boys' Brigade which had its annual camp in the area, the remainder was small indeed. The service was conducted by Canon Verschoyle, the lessons were read by Mr Harvey, and the singing was led by Mrs Harvey at the harmonium. Their voices and manner were, without any affectation, those of the English upper class. Like the small parish church, with its square tower and bells, they could have fitted into any of those areas that were still coloured red on the globes of the 1920s; there they would have been accepted by the people who mattered, and treated with deference by the rest. (Not that such persons were necessarily arrogant. By no means all of them *demanded* deference, but they got it anyway; history saw to that.) For some reason, however, the Harveys, or more probably their ancestors, had chosen to live in Ireland, and they stayed there out of affection or habit long after the tide of empire had ebbed.

As you cycled down the main street of Courtown, the buildings stopped after a hundred yards. You continued across an empty space for another twenty yards, and then you were at the stone wall overlooking the harbour. From the left the Oonavara river flowed into the basin; on the right the channel turned round a corner and went out to sea. Across the harbour stood an old lifeboat house, no longer in use; and, built into the walls of the channel, about eighty yards before it reached the sea, were two massive wooden gates, which used to be closed, and then opened at low tide, allowing the accumulated river water to rush out to sea. This, it was hoped, would clear away the sand which tended to gather across the harbour mouth. The system was never satisfactory, and by now only a few smallish trawlers, like the *Saint Mary*, used the harbour. The larger boats worked out of Arklow, some twenty miles to the north. For most of the year Courtown was a quiet, rather run-down place. But with its stone harbour (made, no doubt, by the same engineers who built the bridge at Ballymoney) and its low slate-roofed buildings, it somehow looked right, like a natural feature of the landscape. In July and August it came to life as holiday-makers from Dublin filled its guest-houses and hotels. Scores of people trooped onto the beach; swam, rowed, or played golf; and then returned for hearty lunches and high teas. At night there were impromptu concerts in the saloons of the Bayview, Bolger's, and the Taravie. (No one knew when the final 'w' had fallen off.) On the harbour-front, next to the Taravie, was a small dance-hall with a four-piece band. It used to become hot and crowded, but many people were sorry when it closed and a much larger, more impersonal place opened further up the road. The new place had pink stucco walls; one of those crystal balls hung from the roof, and a spotlight played on it when the hall was darkened for a slow waltz. Tony and I danced, drank, sang, and generally messed about in Courtown, once or twice a week, for about eight summers. I never once saw a fight; crime was virtually non-existent, and of course no one had even heard of drugs.

After the war Ballymoney seemed to be returning to normal. But that, of course, was an illusion; for 'normal' could only have meant 'as it was in the 1930s'. By 1950 a number of houses in the area had running water and electric light. Contact with the outside world began to increase. A portable radio made it possible to hear, though not very clearly, the ripe Hampshire voice of John Arlott as he described the feats of Lindwall and Miller – and of Bradman, now at the close of his historic career. Later would come the three W's, Walcott, Weekes, and Worrall, with calypso accompaniment: 'Cricket, lovely cricket'. England, for her part, looked to Hutton, Compton and Bedser. Test match commentaries were all we listened to, partly because the poor reception ruled out concerts and plays, partly because we cared little for political discussions and current affairs. (At least we had grasped the truth that politics exists for cricket, not *vice versa*.) In the war years, on Sundays, local people would come to Ballymoney in horse-drawn vehicles, on bicycles, or on foot. They would arrive about noon, spend the afternoon on the far shore, and be gone by 6.30. Unlike casual holidaymakers, they were often quite formally dressed, the women in frocks, shoes and stockings, the men in dark blue suits with light-coloured caps and polished boots. Ridiculously, young people like Tony, Joan and myself used to look on them as visitors. After 1945 cars began to appear in greater numbers. We were, after all, only two hours from Dublin, and places nearer the city were beginning to become crowded. A petrol pump appeared outside the Post Office. Changes took place on the road leading to the beach. Gaps would appear in the hedge, and every few years a new house or bungalow would go up. Then, at some stage, the road itself was covered with tar.

In 1950 these changes were just beginning. Much that was most attractive remained as before. There were still very few houses on Tara Hill; the view from the top had not been blotted out by carelessly planted conifers; and as the clouds passed over it they cast shadows of grey, purple and dark green. From Castletown to Courtown the beaches and headlands were totally unspoilt. People, too, simply by being who they were, would assert the claims of continuity – the Reids, who kept a small shop at the bottom of the road, Pat Connors, who rebuilt the Bungalow in 1953, and Mary Pigeon who helped for many years to keep it going. At the Cross, Mrs Spencer and her family ran the Post Office, combined with a grocery store, with the utmost efficiency and good humour. But 1951 seems a good point to end this account, partly because in the autumn of that year I began a job in England, and partly because in the summer an episode took place which had such frightening possibilities that it seemed to represent a kind of punctuation mark. Early in July Tony and I acquired a small sailing craft that was quite different in design from the dinghy. It was somewhat longer, with a narrower beam and a higher mast. And it carried a jib as well as a mainsail. According to the wooden nameplate screwed to the stern, its name was *Tarka*. Trials at Ballymoney showed it was faster than the dinghy, but also trickier to handle. A

week or so after the boat arrived, I went to London for an (unsuc-
cessful) interview. On my return I heard to my horror that Tony
and a young ten-year-old friend had been almost a mile off shore
when the mainsheet became fouled and the boat capsized. For a
while they clung to the hull, but it gave them little support, and
soon they realized they were being blown farther out to sea. So
each grabbed an oar and began to swim slowly towards the beach.
Since the wind was offshore, their chances of making it were slim.
But providentially (for Providence always gets credit for the happy
things) the accident was seen by Mr Jack Whelan, who was painting the roof of a house. He raised the alarm; the only boat available was launched (without rowlocks); and, eventually, when they
were still over half a mile from shore, the two lads were rescued.
They had been in the water for nearly an hour.

What followed was an anti-climax, but not without oddity. The
papers reported that an Aer Lingus pilot had spotted a boat floating upside-down some miles off the Welsh coast. From that height
no one could tell how large a craft it was or whether there were
any survivors. So the pilot radioed the boat's position, and the
lifeboat from Pwllheli in North Wales put out. According to the
Daily Mail, a Spitfire, a Wellington and two submarines joined in
the search. Conditions were good, but it was still quite a feat to
locate the half-submerged boat, which was eventually brought
ashore. Tony immediately notified the papers that the occupants
were safe. A few days later, when returning from another interview, I went to Caernarvon and then took a bus along that beautiful coast road. After fifteen minutes' walk on a hot summer day I
was standing beside the lifeboat house looking down at the contraption which had so nearly killed my two friends. The oars, of
course, were missing. But apart from that it looked much the same
as when, on the other side of the Irish Sea, it had dumped the two
lads in the water. The boat had now been impounded by the
authorities, and I would have to sign a statement of ownership.
Did I want it back? 'Not on your life!' I said. 'I'm only too pleased
to leave it. But what about all the trouble and expense? And what
about the aircraft and two submarines? How on earth can we pay
them back?' 'I wouldn't worry too much about that. Those boyos
are always looking for something to do, and it gave them a bit of

exercise. As for us here on the lifeboat, well it's our job, isn't it?' That didn't seem quite adequate. But in the end we agreed that the little boat would be auctioned (for use in sheltered waters) and that the proceeds go to the lifeboat fund. I added ten pounds as a thank-offering to Neptune, resolving privately to get half of it back from my partner. Then, when no one was looking, I took a sixpence and unscrewed the wooden plate with the name *Tarka* on it. Forty years later, the name-plate stands like a votive-tablet on my cousin's mantlepiece in Cornwall.

Dublin

The worst you could say of Dublin in the war years was that it was drab and run down. Little new construction was done, and many buildings fell into disrepair. Transport services became skeletal – in places almost ghostly, and certain shortages were acute. (The tea ration, for instance, was half an ounce a week, and coal was not to be had.) In pro-British circles it seemed to be assumed these privations were simply the inevitable result of wartime conditions. I never heard it suggested that they were in any way connected with British policy. That, however, may just have been my ignorance. Others, doubtless, knew the truth, namely that from early 1941, to make sure that Eire should not be both neutral *and* comfortable, the British Cabinet imposed a series of trade sanctions. As a result, Eire's imports of fertilizer from Britain fell from 74,000 tons in 1940 to 7000 in 1941 and to zero in 1942. The petrol supplies of 1940 were halved in 1941 and reduced by a further quarter in 1942. In the same period imports of gas coal fell from 3500 tons a week to 1600.[11] This last reduction led to gas being shut off in Dublin during certain hours of the day; but if you lived in a fairly high area you could do a little surreptitious cooking on 'the glim'. Spot checks were therefore carried out by 'the glimmer man', who, if one believed *Dublin Opinion*, regularly burnt his fingers by testing people's gas stoves. One housewife answered a ring at the door at 11 a.m. and found a lady on her doorstep. 'Thanks be to God,' she said, 'I thought you were the glimmer man!' 'Well, you've spoken too soon, I'm the glimmer woman.'

In the first two years of the war a few bombs fell on Dublin. Much the worst incident took place in May 1941, when 34 people

127

were killed in the North Strand, 90 were injured, and 300 houses were wrecked or damaged. The official explanation, apparently accepted by both Britain and Germany, was that the Luftwaffe had been misled by British interference with their radio beams.[12] Maybe. But if the pilots believed they were over an English or Welsh city, they must have been pleasantly surprised at the inefficiency of the black-out. As for the two major raids on Belfast, it was widely known in the south that fire-engines (13 in all) from Dún Laoghaire, Dublin, Drogheda and Dundalk had helped to fight the blaze, thus lending extra point to the question 'I know we're neutral, but who are we neutral against?' But thanks to the censorship imposed by the government, solid and detailed information was hard to come by. After the war a scholar investigating the matter found that, in both Belfast and Dublin, official records had been unaccountably mislaid.[13] In other questions, too, concerning the war, rumours took the place of information. But one could always choose which rumours to believe. We never believed that U-boats were secretly refuelled off Donegal or the south-west coast, partly because we didn't *want* to believe it, partly because it seemed unlikely that Irishmen could supply diesel fuel to the Germans when they had hardly any for themselves. It seems that our scepticism was justified. According to Fisk, in a few cases Irish fishermen sold their catch to U-boats, and even more rarely U-boat crews came ashore to obtain food.[14] But such acts were certainly not connived at by the government. On the other hand we were happy to believe stories about the repatriation of allied aircrew. Here credulity rather than scepticism has been vindicated; for it is now known that several dozen individuals, including an American general, were sent across the border to Ulster.[15] On other matters our opinions were less close to the truth. While we were largely unaware of the constant efforts made by Sir John Maffey (the British Representative) and Mr David Gray (the US Minister) to persuade de Valéra to abandon neutrality and come in on the Allied side, we probably overestimated the activities of Dr Hempel (the German Minister), assuming that he was actively promoting German espionage and encouraging the maximum amount of German interference. Readers of Enno Stephan's book now realize that there was no network of German spies in Ireland,

and that the operations which did take place were sometimes comically ineffective.[16] What, then, of espionage on the side of Britain? My people would hardly have understood the question: surely, it only makes sense to spy on an *enemy*? Still, acquiring information is close to 'gathering intelligence', which shades into 'engaging in espionage'. Sending confidential reports about the Irish leaders and Irish opinion to the British Ministry of Information is surely *one* kind of thing that secret agents do, though few spies have commanded the elegant style and the effortless assurance of Miss Elizabeth Bowen. Yet in the purely military sense it is hard to believe that such reports were of much significance. Certainly, as a centre for international intrigue, Dublin could not compare with Lisbon, Stockholm or Berne – to say nothing of Ankara and Istanbul. As Bernard Share so charmingly put it, 'one of the many problems besetting the spies in Ireland was that there was very little to spy on.'[17]

If, about 1946, you had leant on the parapet of O'Connell Bridge and looked up river, you would have seen the quays with their second-hand bookshops, the stylish curve of the metal bridge, the Capel Street bridge, and the green dome of Gandon's Four Courts. The scene would have been much the same as that depicted in one of Bartlett's engravings, except that instead of his slim, almost Venetian boats, you might have seen one of Guinness's barges puffing towards you and lowering its red funnel as it passed underneath the bridge. The crew used to wear navy jerseys and peaked caps; and up at the wharf, where the barrels were loaded for their journey downstream to the cargo ships, they assumed the air of seasoned mariners bound for distant ports. Somewhere in Joyce, I think, a Dubliner leans over the wall as the barge is casting off and shouts, 'Hey mister, bring us back a parrot, will ye?' The cargo ships, and also the old B&I passenger-boats to Liverpool, would make their way down river, past the Alexandra Basin, and then, leaving the Clontarf inlet to port, would sail between two lighthouses out into Dublin Bay.

On leaving school, I went to live with the Poldens in Victoria Road, Clontarf, where my Uncle Stan kindly gave me a room. Lodebar, a Hebrew name which was supposed to mean 'without pasture' was a solid Victorian semi. As it faced north, it got rather little sunshine. The best view was from the third-floor lavatory window at the back. When you lowered the upper sash, with its frosted glass, you could see south across the inlet to the Alexandra Basin, where a large merchant vessel, interned for the duration of 'the emergency', lay quietly rusting. Left of that stood the chimneys of the Pigeon House electricity station. And behind that, beyond the south-eastern suburbs, was the magnificent backdrop of the Dublin Mountains.

S.E. Polden, who was cashier in the Ballast Office on O'Connell Bridge, never earned more than £600 a year. True, he had no worries about a mortgage, since Lodebar was a wedding-present from James H. Cooke. He also grew some of his own vegetables and fruit, and had a hen-run at the bottom of the garden. He did not smoke or drink. And he kept a careful record of his expenses. (He was the only man I ever knew who, when he opened a new razor-blade, marked the date on the little envelope.) Nevertheless, on that salary he was able to maintain a bungalow in Ballymoney, educate three children and put the eldest through Trinity, run a car, and employ a maid. He had a large joint of meat sent up from Redmond's of Gorey every week, and he regularly travelled to Britain with the Irish rugby team. None of this will surprise older readers, who recall that the fare from Clontarf to Nelson's Pillar was tuppence; eggs cost a shilling a dozen; prime beef cost two shillings a pound; a pint of porter could be had for eight pence; a cinema seat cost one and six; and the name of The Fifty Shilling Tailors was only a little out of date. I remember feeling acutely embarrassed when, in 1949, my host paid six and sixpence (i.e. just over 30p) each for four very good dinners at the Moira, a small hotel and restaurant run by Jury's.

I am not enough of an economist to know whether a low cost of living is always accompanied by widespread poverty. But that certainly was the case in Dublin. One of the poor was Aunt Connie's daily help, Molly Egan, who was by now in her late sixties. I have no idea what she was paid (perhaps as little as two shillings a day). But she also got presents of cast-off clothes and various items of food, including bowls of dripping. Nowadays this sounds horribly patronizing, but then it counted as no more than a decent gesture and no one thought anything about it. One day I was asked to deliver a parcel containing a bowl of dripping to Molly's little house in Brian Boru Street behind the tram sheds on Clontarf Road. As I was leaving, Aunt Connie called, 'Oh, and as you're passing Mrs Cox's, perhaps you'd give her back that package of *Country Life*; it's on the hall table.' Now Mrs Cox was a rather smart widow who lived on Castle Avenue. Her son was a District Officer with the Colonial Service in Uganda, and although she was very friendly and often accompanied my mother and aunt to watch rugby, you could tell from her accent that she was a notch or two above us. Anyhow, I duly set off, but the goddess of Farce presided over my journey; for I delivered *Country Life* to Molly Egan and the bowl of dripping to Mrs Cox. I made sure I was somewhere else when the wires were uncrossed.

Though our health was looked after by Uncle Willie, there was no dentist in the family, and so Joan and I were taken at first to Mr Wigoder in Harcourt Street. In spite of his odious profession, I rather liked him, for after filling your tooth he would take out a large round tin of toffees and let you choose one '... and one to take away. But remember, chew on the other side!' I never encountered this rather dubious practice anywhere else. Subsequently we went to an old schoolmate of my father's, who kept a pedal-drill in his surgery. 'What's that?' I asked uneasily. 'Ah well, you see, every Wednesday I hold a surgery down in Athy; so I just throw the old drill into the back of the car. Very handy. But here, of course, we have the latest thing!' patting a large chromium crane-like contraption which seemed to be driven by a pair of rubber bands. No doubt the electric drill marked a great advance, but it certainly did not eliminate pain. In fact one just accepted pain fatalistically as part of a visit to the dentist's. A few years after the war an English undergraduate in Trinity asked me if I knew a good dentist. 'Of course,' I said automatically, and gave him Mr Hart's phone number. A week later he came up to me in the Front Square. 'What do you mean by sending me to that brute of a dentist? I've never endured such agony. He didn't even give me an injection for my filling!' 'B-but surely *no* one gives an injection for a filling.' 'My dear Niall, just because you're a classicist there's no need to make a cult of the antique. Next time I'll ask someone else.' After that, I saw Mr Hart in a new light. On one of my later visits, before I left Dublin, he told me that he always operated on his own teeth, which suggested that he was not only a sadist but also a masochist – and a contortionist too.

I ought not to have been so naive about dentists, for a few years earlier, when home on holiday, I had a nasty experience with another kind of surgeon. It had started with a sore throat. Uncle Willie said, 'Open wide'. Then, pressing my tongue down with a teaspoon, he said, 'Say, "Ah".' I did. 'Yes, the old tonsils are infected. I'll get C.V. Telford to take them out. He's a first class chap; one of our top men. In three or four days you'll be as right as rain. Before then you may have to eat ice-cream, but *you* won't mind that, eh?' Remembering my appendix operation in Belfast, I assumed I would be totally unconscious throughout. In the event, though rather dopey, I distinctly felt them insert a gag between my teeth. I saw Telford bend over me. Then came two agonizing jerks, whereupon I sat up on the operating-table and poured blood into a strategically placed pail. Meanwhile, C.V. Telford, doubtless a busy man, was putting on his jacket. As he went out the door he waved cheerfully, 'Goodbye Neil!' Blast him, he couldn't even get my name right.

In the years after the war, when cars reappeared, you bought a licence across the counter for ten shillings. No one was tactless enough to ask whether you could actually drive. Nor did anyone try to ensure that vehicles were roadworthy. The car that Uncle Stan bought at this time was a 1934 Citroen, a model which gave no hint of the company's excellent post-war designs. It hated starting, and once under way it could not exceed 35 mph; which was just as well, for, as Ralph Nader said about a later vehicle, it was unsafe at any speed. The Polden boys had by now left home; Uncle Stan did not drive, and Joan was just learning. So I did duty as the family chauffeur. As such, I was constantly amazed by the sheer variety of the car's mechanical failures. The worst moment came when we drove to a rugby international. Uncle Stan had a permit which allowed the car to be taken into the ground. So I turned into Lansdowne Road, moving slowly, for spectators were walking in the middle of the roadway. As we neared the level crossing the crowd became thicker, and I inched along in first gear. Then, just as we were going up the ramp to cross the tracks, the gates swung across and clanged shut immediately in front of the bonnet. So, you say, why not put on the handbrake and wait? Unfortunately, the handbrake was useless, and even the footbrake, for some reason, did not work properly in reverse. I was afraid to shut off and leave the car in gear for fear it would never start again. So I decided to hold it in first with the clutch slipping. People were now packed tightly on each side and behind us. Once when I rolled back six inches an angry face appeared at the window. 'Will you watch where you're driving! Do you want to kill the people?' After what seemed an age the train passed through and the gates opened. I swung the car into the ground; and then, just as I had parked it against the wall, the accelerator pedal snapped clean off. For weeks afterwards I used to wake up, stamping frantically on the board at the foot of my bed. Then, to everyone's relief, my uncle decided to get another car.

If you had been in Howth or Dún Laoghaire on a summer evening in the late 40s you would have seen the sails of the Mermaids, the Seventeens, and the Twenty-one-footers, competing as they had for years. Some of the classes were very old. The Wags, indeed, were said to go back to the end of the nineteenth century. We were not a boating family, and I could not afford to buy anything for myself. So, like many students, I crewed for other people on an irregular *ad hoc* basis – usually in small boats like Fourteen-foot International Dinghies or Fireflies. The only time when I crewed on a larger craft, the trip ended in a tragic accident. Desmond O'Hanlon, a dermatologist and a member of a well-known medical family, decided to spend ten days of his holidays racing *Evora* (a cruiser of about twenty-five feet) in a series of regattas in the Menai Straits. As he wanted a fourth member for the crew, he kindly took me with him. On about the fifth evening we were anchored just off the harbour at Caernarvon. Soon after 11 p.m. Desmond rowed a guest ashore. An hour later I felt the dinghy bump into the side of the boat and heard Desmond's voice call out. I quickly went on deck, where I was joined by the other two. What followed cannot have taken more than a minute. Desmond said he had lost an oar, and asked for a rope so that he could pull the dinghy alongside. We flung him a rope, which he grabbed hold of. But such was the force of the tidal race that he was immediately swept astern. Had he been able to make fast the rope to the bow of the dinghy and then sit in the stern, all might perhaps have been well. But this proved impossible. He could only stand in the bow holding the rope. Within seconds the bow was forced under and the dinghy began to fill. He then came out of the dinghy on the end of the rope. We called to him to hold on while we pulled him in. But the strain must have been too great, for he let go and was carried away into the darkness. Sadly, he was a non-swimmer and was not wearing a life-jacket.

The emotional effect of the accident was probably quite normal; but, as I had never experienced anything similar, I remember thinking it rather odd. Mentally I remained quite dispassionate. I realized at once that Desmond was gone; yet it seemed indecent to do nothing. So I started the engine, the others pulled up the anchor, and we set off with the current towards the north-east, calling out and shining a lamp on the surface of the water. After half an hour of this operation, which we all knew to be quite futile, we returned to Caernarvon, and, having no dinghy, we tied up beside a cargo ship at the quayside. Later at the police station I was still quite lucid and almost detached, and was able to dictate an account of the accident. (The others, of course, did the same.) Then, as I started out for the hotel where we had booked in, I realized that physically I was so exhausted that I could barely walk. When I eventually got home I fell onto a bed and slept for sixteen hours.

Tennis could be enjoyed without such trauma. For some years I played, with minimal success, in the schools' championships at Fitzwilliam. The tournament was run by Mr A.P. MacWeeney (a well-known sports journalist) and Mr Michael Barry. Goodness knows why they did it, for the headaches must have been numerous. But one day in the club-house I caught a glimpse of how they operated. MacWeeney, a large portly man wearing a half-sleeve shirt and carrying a glass of whiskey, came out of the office looking rather disgruntled. 'Micky, will you tell the little bastards they can't just bugger off when they feel like it; they've bloody well got to come and see *me*.' Mr Barry, a thin ascetic-looking figure in a grey suit, with a circle of fuzzy hair around his pale head, and a thick pair of glasses, moved quietly to the microphone. The message, chanted in an ecclesiastical monotone, emerged transmuted: 'Competitors are requested not to leave the ground without consulting Mr MacWeeney.' Periodically the same voice would instruct players to get ready. Some of the names come floating back after nearly half a century: 'Rachel Blair-White, change please; Renée de Laforcade, change please; Thaddeus Courtney, change please.' Such names indicate the more glamorous end of our social spectrum. But the Dublin that my friends and I knew, though fuzzy at the edges, was yet rather limited. I was never a guest at any of the large country houses, and never rode to hounds. Equally, I had no conception of what life was like on a small farm or in a Dublin tenement. Still, there was a good deal of variety within the expanding middle class, and it offered more fun than might have been expected from a social group whose chief values were supposed to be security, respectability, and comfort. As you turned left outside the Front Gate of Trinity, you would wave to X – you played rugger with *him*, or greet Y – you sailed or played tennis with *him*, or stopped to chat with Z – you had sung or danced or acted (but almost certainly had never slept) with *her*. Perhaps because it was a middling group in a relatively small city, one had the impression of knowing a large number of people. At Christmas time especially it seemed impossible to walk down Grafton Street without meeting a dozen friends. And with the bright windows and coloured lights and the groups of carol-singers the whole place held an atmosphere of cheerfulness and excitement.

Christmas, in Dublin as elsewhere, brought performances of *The Messiah*. The Clontarf singers, organized and conducted by Dorothy Graham, presented their version about 1948 in the Metropolitan Hall. It had two interesting features: first, one of the soloists was the distinguished tenor Richard Lewis (which showed that our wartime isolation was behind us), and secondly, the choir was accompanied not by an orchestra or an organ, but by two pianos. Though this decision was taken for practical reasons, the effect was quite illuminating, for it brought out many of the intricacies in Handel's writing which are normally overwhelmed in a sea of sound. Such occasions brought us into touch, in however marginal a way, with the musical life of Dublin. At the centre of that life were a number of somewhat eccentric individuals. At the final rehearsal for a performance of *The Creation*, to be given in the church at Clontarf, the bass-baritone, Mr Brian Boydell, asked Dorothy Graham about dress. 'Oh, a nice dark suit of some kind will do splendidly, Brian.' 'Jolly good.' At the performance, as we were moving to our places in the choir, Boydell appeared. 'I found a nice dark suit, Dorothy, but I thought it needed something to brighten it up.' He was wearing a yellow tie. And when he took his seat in the front it became clear that he was also wearing a pair of fur-lined flying boots.

Concerts, plays, sport – these were the meshes which held our rather loose network together. Also important were the newspapers, especially *The Irish Times*. This had been traditionally a Protestant pro-British paper, reflecting the interests of the Anglo-Irish. After the Treaty of 1921 it was clear that if the paper wanted to survive it would have to become a lot less Anglo and a lot more Irish. This shift in balance was mainly the achievement of the editor, R.M. Smyllie, a man 'who wore a green sombrero, weighed twenty-two stone, sang parts of his leading articles in operatic recitative, and grew the nail on his little finger into the shape of a pen nib, like Keats'.[18] During the war, in addition to the routine worries of editing a daily paper, Smyllie had to cope with a strict censorship imposed by the government. Most people failed to realize the problems and frustrations that this involved. Here are a few sentences from his leader of 12 May 1945, written with passion on the day after censorship had been lifted:

It is difficult – indeed, it is impossible – to write with moderation about the treatment which this newspaper has received from the censorship during recent years. Alone among the Dublin dailies, we have been compelled to submit to the autocrats of Dublin Castle every line that we proposed to print, from the leading article down to the humblest prepaid advertisement. We always were careful to say nothing that might prejudice either the Government's policy of neutrality or the maintenance of public order; yet it was seldom indeed that our leading articles were not hacked and mutilated in such a way as to make them almost meaningless. Shoals of letters have reached this office from time to time accusing us of pro-Axis leanings; obviously the writers had no conception of the way in which our mouths were muzzled. Now, thank God, the censorship is gone.[19]

In addition to his leaders, R.M. Smyllie would contribute to the column headed 'An Irishman's Diary' under the name of Nichevo. Here he recounted snippets of gossip about notabilities whom *he* always seemed to know, recalled stories about Ruhleben (the German prison camp where he had been interned in the first world war), told golfing anecdotes picked up in Delgany (a picturesque golf course in Co. Wicklow), and passed on chit-chat that came his way in the Pearl Bar. It was all presented in a rather knowing old-boy manner and garnished with Latin tags. A typical item might have gone something like this:

My old friend Charles Cream, the Surgeon-General, dropped in last Wednesday. Now that he has finished re-organizing the RAMC he intends to spend more time in his native Sligo. The same bold Charlie is a dab hand with rod and line, and a little bird tells me he has in mind a *pied à terre* not a million miles from Lough Arrow. As students he and Bethel Solomons always ran neck and neck for the glittering prizes (*Arcades ambo*). But whereas he went off to serve King and country Bethel stayed in Dublin to the eternal gratitude of countless mothers. Charles Cream, of course, is a son of Sir Redvers, the Governor of Mysore, who alas is no longer with us. *Sic transit gloria mundi.* He was one of the giant race before the flood.

Another writer in the same column was Patrick Campbell, whose pen-name was Quidnunc. Immensely tall, with a fringe of red hair, and a stammer which he managed to turn into a social asset, Campbell later became familiar to readers of the *Sunday Dispatch* and then to TV audiences. But in the 40s he was already well known in Ireland, especially in golfing circles. One story, which I have reason to believe, concerned a weekend with a group at Rosse's Point. After some heavy potations the night before, a foursome walked rather gingerly to the first tee. As Campbell was preparing to drive, a small blue butterfly alighted on his ball. Without any sign of distraction, Campbell swung through the ball and sent a huge drive zooming down the fairway. The others were awed by his concentration, and one of them said, 'Did the butterfly not put you off?' 'I-I say. Do you m-mean it was really there?' At some stage it must have been pointed out that an Irish *woman* would also have something to contribute to the Diary. So Candida joined the team, talking to visitors and telling her readers what women were doing in the arts, business, and the professions. In 1950 (by which time Seamus Kelly had taken over from Patrick Campbell), R.B.D. French wrote a skit on the trio for the Trinity College pantomime. It started:

> We're Candida, Quidnunc, and Nichevo,
> The people you all want to meet.
> We're the sauce and the caper,
> The spice of the paper,
> The gossips of Westmoreland Street.
>
> We're the Argus, the sentry, the scout,
> And we watch all your goings about.
>
> We know to a pin
> Just who wants to get in -
> And those that we want to keep out!

There were also other reasons for taking *The Irish Times*. Some readers were addicted to 'Cruiskeen Lawn', written by Myles na gCopaleen, *alias* Flann O'Brien, author of *At Swim-Two-Birds*, *alias* Brian O'Nolan, ex-civil-servant, satirist, talker, and drinker. Others enjoyed the correspondence columns, where current affairs, including questions of morality and religion, were debated with a wit and astringency not often encountered in the English dailies. Others again would glance at the 'hatches, matches and dispatches', simply to keep in touch with 'the people we know'.

What follows is largely a collection of student reminiscences. But as many students in those years came from the North of Ireland, and as I, in a sense, was one of them, I will say something here about The North. (The reader who is thoroughly fed up with the whole topic should skip this paragraph.) I suggested earlier that the difference between Catholics and Protestants in Northern Ireland had little to do with theology *per se*. From, say, 1940–65, the situation was altogether quieter than it has been since 1970; and yet the same purely theological differences were also present then. Moreover, not only do both sides accept the main tenets of the Christian creed (the incarnation, the atonement, and the resurrection) – tenets which bring them together in a single group, and mark them off from hundreds of millions of their contemporaries – but most people in the North have little knowledge of the finer points on which the two denominations differ. In the doctrine of transubstantiation, for instance, both sides believe that the bread and wine, blessed and served at communion, are bread and wine in the ordinary sense; i.e. that if tested in any laboratory they would prove to be bread and wine. Catholics believe that, over and above the ordinary sense, the bread and wine are *metaphysically* the body and blood of Christ. Protestants believe that, over and above the ordinary sense, the bread and wine are *symbolically* the body and blood of Christ. Such divergencies are surely of marginal importance. But where religious differences carry political and, more especially, social and economic implications, that is where the trouble starts; for after Partition Ulster Catholics rightly feared that, in the areas where they were more numerous, political boundaries would be re-drawn; that where housing was scarce they would be at the end of the list; that in government, industry and the professions they would be less likely to obtain important posts; that when the economy began to falter they would be the first to lose their jobs; and that on the festivals of the Orange Order they would be annually insulted. Protestants, with equal justice, were afraid that if a Catholic majority emerged in Ulster, Stormont would vote Northern Ireland out of the United Kingdom into the Republic; then the British subsidy would be removed and Ulster's prosperity would suffer accordingly. Moreover, because of the power of the Catholic Church, birth control, divorce and cremation would be forbidden; in dangerous births, the mother's life would be sacrificed to save the child; children of mixed marriages would have to be raised as Catholics; and everyone would be subject to censorship and have to learn Irish. No improvement can be expected until these fears, which have led to the crisis of the past quarter of a century, are substantially reduced.

In 1946 these problems were a cloud no bigger than a red hand. Only a pessimist would have predicted what happened in the 70s and 80s. In Trinity College, during the immediate post-war years, Ulster students supplied over 25 per cent of the population, including some of the best scholars and athletes; and they contributed notably to the diversity of college life. All periods, no doubt, are periods of transition, but at that time it was easy to identify certain prominent features that belonged to the past, and also certain forces that were bound to bring change. As part of their victory celebrations in 1945 a group of pro-British hotheads hoisted the Union Jack on the roof above the Front Gate. (The Irish flag was flown in a subordinate position.) An equally hotheaded group of anti-British students gathered in College Green. There are conflicting reports about what happened next, but at any rate emotions got out of hand and in the course of the disturbance, the Irish tricolour was burnt. This episode, for which Provost Alton had to apologize to de Valéra, confirmed the belief, held in many quarters, that Trinity College was still an alien, indeed anti-Irish, institution; and it gave ammunition to those who wanted to wind the place up and drive a road right through the middle. Another event, which was equally backward-looking in its implications, had taken place a few years before. That was the proclamation by John Charles McQuaid, Catholic Archbishop of Dublin, that it was a mortal sin for any of his flock to attend Trinity College without his personal dispensation. A mortal sin. Just think what that means. The authors of a very informative and entertaining history of the College say that the ban was shown to have been ineffective by the fact that the percentage of Catholics rose to 23 in 1950.[20] But that point in itself, without further details, does not fully convince; for the increase could have come from Catholics who were not under the Archbishop's authority. In any case, a few years later, there was a ludicrous sequel. For when the College, in an effort to be more liberal and ecumenical, approached the Archbishop requesting the appointment of a Catholic Chaplain, permission was refused. Another absurdity (to complete the triad of politics, religion and sex) was the six o'clock rule, i.e. that women were not allowed in College after 6 p.m. But what about evening meetings of an educative kind? And, more serious still, what about the library? Surely women students could not be barred from the reading-room? To get round these difficulties the authorities excogitated a new form of double-entry book-keeping. Each woman had to sign a book in the porter's lodge at Front Gate, stating the exact time of entry; then, after crossing the Front Square, she would sign a second book on arrival at the reading-room. The two books were regularly compared, and any discrepancy would lead to a stern enquiry from Dr Kenneth Claude Bailey, the Junior

Dean. Dr Bailey's vigilance was also displayed on the occasion when students applied for permission to play mixed squash. He hurried down to inspect the courts, found that a minute area of floor could not be observed from the spectators' gallery, and immediately refused the request. 'Anything could go on down there. Anything!' As Aldous Huxley said, to the puritan all things are impure.

Nevertheless, changes were afoot. October 1946 brought a huge increase in numbers. Over half of the new freshmen were born in Great Britain, and a significant fraction came from overseas. Rather callow youngsters, like myself, who had come off the school assembly-line, found themselves mingling with veterans of the 14th Army or Bomber Command, or with former GIs. Such people wore various items of military uniform, occasionally for warmth. Every now and then they would 'take a shufti' or 'carry out a recce'; they might find themselves mixed up in 'a shaky do', but would 'press on regardless', and eventually 'hit the sack'. In approval they would exclaim 'bang on!', 'good show!', 'I rather care for that!' When fed up, they might dismiss 'the top brass' as 'an absolute shower'. And sometimes they encouraged each other with the maxim *illegitimis non carborundum*, which was supposed to mean 'don't let the bastards grind you down'. A few went in for heavy drinking and wild parties, but many were more serious than they let on. Whereas conventional students would try to fit their experience, as they acquired it, into an evolving intellectual framework, the ex-servicemen already had enough experience to be going on with. They now wanted an intellectual framework which would help them to make sense of it.

Internally too, the College was on the verge of change. The staff had been severely depleted during the war; the average age of the Senior Fellows was now nearly seventy; buildings had fallen into disrepair; equipment was out of date. So by the autumn of 1946 ideas, money and personnel were urgently needed. Some signs of recovery were apparent when, in 1947, de Valéra agreed to provide an annual grant of £35,000, and a new batch of Fellows was elected. Still, the Junior Fellows were by now organizing themselves into a pressure group, convinced that, to meet the new conditions, the whole power-structure of the College would have to be changed. Plans or plots, depending on which side you took, were already being worked out in the late 40s and some preliminary manoeuvres were taking place.[21] Yet remarkably little of all this was revealed to the students. In my own department, for instance, the staff, it seems, was divided between those committed to change, those who were dragging their feet, and those who were firmly in favour of the *status quo*. Yet the gentlemanly code prevailed, and on the principle of 'not in front of the children' no academic ever criticized his colleagues. This did not prevent us forming opinions of our own on some of the more obvious issues. For instance, it was clear even to freshmen, who talk freely amongst themselves, that for one reason or another there were relatively few academics of distinction on the College staff, and that this situation was not helped by the long-standing practice of appointing potentially productive scholars to posts like those of Registrar and Librarian – posts which were full-time jobs in themselves and for which scholars might not necessarily have the right qualities.

These were large general matters, at some distance from the student's immediate concern. But within his department or school he might well have encountered a similar mixture of archaic and progressive features. There he came to know such issues in detail; and because they affected his welfare and his way of life, he felt keenly about them. One traditional feature of the School of Classics became apparent at the orals for Sizarship in the summer of 1946. Here I met Norman Rodway, who had been a year behind me at High School. He proved to have not only a wide intellectual range but also an excellent memory which would serve him well when he took up acting. As we sat waiting apprehensively for our first *viva* (on Thucydides, Book 2), it became clear that the Headmaster of High School, Mr John Bennett, was closely familiar with the Trinity system and had prepared his pupil well. For, noticing that Norman had two or three Greek words written at the top of every page of his text, I said, 'What are those for?' 'Oh,' he said, 'Stanford has a slip of paper with a list of words in Greek; he'll ask what they mean.' 'Oh God,' I said, and seized his text. 'What on earth is that word – *phruktos*?' 'Oh, that's a beacon-fire.' 'And what about that, and that, and that?' We had gone through about half a dozen words when my name was called and I walked up to the dais where a strikingly handsome man was sitting. He had gun-metal hair and piercing blue eyes, and wore a grey-blue suit. In a bored Hiberno-English voice he asked me to translate part of Thucydides' description of the plague at Athens. Then he pushed a slip of paper in front of me. 'Translate those six words, please.' I remembered about four. 'Well then, to make up for what you missed, can you tell me the meaning of *phruktos*?' I swallowed hard and said, 'I believe it's a beacon-fire.' 'You believe correctly. Kindly have Mr Rodway come up.' Twenty minutes later, Norman rejoined me. 'Well, how did it go?' Rodway ground his teeth. 'Confound him anyway! He asked me what *phruktos* was and I couldn't remember.' An amazing lapse, but in the end it didn't matter, for four of us were accepted.

While W.B. Stanford's *viva*-technique was in certain respects old-fashioned, in two other, far more important, ways he was ahead of his time. First, by 1948 English commentaries on Homer's *Odyssey* were over sixty years out of date. Much work had been done in the inter-war years, but ironically, in England at least, this had promoted the doctrine of unripe time. 'It's much too soon to attempt another general commentary. We haven't decided yet whether Homer was one poet or two. Milman Parry's researches into oral epic have yet to be assimilated. There are still problems in Aegean chronology. And we must await the decipherment of Linear B; that will place the epics in a new light' (it didn't). Stanford had the courage to ignore these misgivings, and write his commentary, which held the field for well over forty years. Secondly, for obscure reasons which can't be discussed here, classical scholars in Britain (with a couple of distinguished exceptions like Gilbert Murray and C.M. Bowra) rarely went in for literary theory or literary criticism. But Stanford wrote on metaphor and style and (taking some hints from William Empson) on ambiguity. A few years later he produced his admirable synthetic study of the Ulysses theme from Homer to Joyce. Such independence was one of the advantages of provincialism.

Stanford's colleague, Herbert Parke, the Professor of Ancient History, though equally distinguished (he was the chief authority on the Delphic Oracle), was different in almost every way. A small wiry man with quick movements and a nervous laugh, he possessed enormous reserves of energy. He had done important war-work in the Ministry of Supply, and in 1949 a few years after returning to Dublin he took on the post of Librarian in addition to his teaching duties. Parke's *vivas*, too, could be disconcerting. He was always embarrassed by ignorance, and after a brief interval he would laugh uneasily and provide the answer himself. After one such session a contemporary of mine returned to his seat and put his head in his hands. 'How was it?' I asked. 'Disaster. Total disaster. Parke did magnificently; answered virtually every question.' Whereas Stanford's classes were surprisingly relaxed affairs, sometimes providing little more than desultory conversation, Parke's lectures were above our heads. His discussion of historical problems reflected the kind of work he had done for Greats, and assumed a good deal of preparation; so too, in describing Greek vase-painting or sculpture, he pursued analogies in medieval and renaissance art which made us groan with despair. This feeling of inadequacy led to a certain amount of juvenile buffoonery. Three minutes before the lecture was due to begin, a pseudo-Parke would enter the room with quick steps, feet slightly turned out and head on one side. Grasping the lectern, he would begin, 'Last time, I suggested that Praxiteles ...' But before he had finished the sentence, another pseudo-Parke would appear saying 'In connection with the François vase ...' There would be just time for a third imposter to say, 'As Beazely once remarked ...', when the original would come through the door. The trouble was that, after three false prophets, one was half inclined to dismiss the man himself as a fake. At first we assumed that our childishness was a matter of age; for while the junior freshmen were drawing cartoons, exchanging limericks, and mimicking the professor, the three years ahead of us sat in their gowns quietly taking notes. But in our final session it became clear that the three years behind us were perfectly respectable, whereas our behaviour was much the same. So we had to draw a less charitable conclusion. However, being a man of generous spirit, Parke did not hold our folly against us. A year or two later, when I had to make up a lot of history quickly for my first job, he was kind enough to lend me his notes.

When R.W. Tate was elected to a Fellowship in 1908 at the age of thirty-six, the College no doubt congratulated itself on making a strong appointment. Tate had taken a first in both parts of the Cambridge Tripos, and in the Fellowship exam he had obtained exceptional marks in Greek and Latin composition (prose and verse). He had an enviable control of French, German, Italian and Russian. He commanded the Officers' Training Corps from 1910–22, except for a wartime break when he was an interpreter (firstclass). He was honoured by the French and Italian governments, and was knighted in 1920. In the context of Edwardian Britain, that was a brilliant career; and it was perfectly complemented by the man's personality. For Tate was tall, aquiline, conservative, ir-ascible, and warm-hearted; a sport and, by all the usual definitions, a gentleman. In my day some older people still remembered his public speeches and his recitations of Kipling and Newbolt at smoking-concerts. Sadly, by the 1940s Sir Robert's professional talents were no longer greatly valued. To be sure, his skill as a composer (seen in his *Carmina Dublinensia*) was admired as an elegant, but entirely marginal, accomplishment; and he was envied for his exceptional verbal memory. But it was clear that his wide reading in many languages had not engendered much in the way of discrimination (he ranked Kipling above most English poets); worse still, he was almost totally devoid of ideas, whether literary of philosophical. Once, after a term's lectures on Plato's *Phaedo* he said, 'Well gentlemen,' (overlooking the presence of two ladies) 'I trust that with the aid of Mr Archer-Hind we have covered all the most important points of language in this absorbing dialogue. As for the philosophy, since I am told that Plato's position does not differ materially from the Christian creed, I have felt justified in leaving it entirely alone.' Oddly, he had an equal contempt for the technical side of scholarship (apart from grammar). Behind his dismissal of 'Housman and his wasps', lay a deep indifference to text-ual investigation. As for papyrology, he once quoted with glee a remark of Tyrrell's about a newly published collection of versions: 'It shows more evidence of true scholarship than the publication of all the washing-lists of Thothnes that ever came out of the sands of Egypt' – a swipe surely originally aimed at Mahaffy. Finally, Sir Robert's expertise in languages never extended to pronunciation. According to R.M. Smyllie, he found it hard to communicate with French waiters; and I remember him admitting with rueful candour that a French lady who was coaching him in conversation concluded, 'Vous savez bien la grammaire, mais vous n'avez pas l'esprit de la langue.' Predictably, he used the unreformed pronunciation of Greek and Latin. He knew this was wrong. 'The Greeks pronounced au, not as aw, but as ow (i.e. as in how). We can be sure of this because the dog in the witness-box in Aristophanes' *Wasps* says au au, and my dog invariably says ow ow.' But not even the dog could persuade him to change his habits.

Although he was far from being an aristocrat (his father was a rector in Co. Leitrim), in his social attitudes Sir Robert reflected life as he knew it at Shrewsbury and Cambridge towards the end of the Victorian era. His assumptions were revealed one day when a student, attending a tutorial in his rooms, relayed a message: 'Sir, the lady who left a few minutes ago said she'd be back later this afternoon.' 'The *lady*? D'ye mean the good woman who cleans the grate?' It should be added, however, that students by definition came on the right side of the line. Simply by being in his classroom we ranked as gentlemen – a quaintly erroneous assumption. But though female students likewise ranked as ladies, that did not mean that they found him any the less frightening. In his later years, being rather hard of hearing, he would say 'My dear young lady, would ye kindly speak up!' Then, if she complied too vigorously, he would immediately rasp, 'No need to *shout*!' In *viva-voce* examinations the strains would sometimes prove too much, and the student would burst into tears. This upset Sir Robert, because it indicated a failure in courtesy on his part. And a rumour developed that he would then appease his conscience by giving her extra marks.

In Trinity, Scholarship was the name given to an exam normally taken in one's second year. If successful, one received free tuition, free commons (i.e. dinner), rooms at half rent, and an annual salary. In 1830 this salary amounted to £18.9.3 per annum. By 1948 it had climbed to a vertiginous £25. That exam was the only occasion on which I had an oral from Sir Robert Tate. As usually happened on these occasions, I was writing an answer on some wholly different topic when I was tapped on the shoulder and a voice said 'He's ready for you.' I went out and knocked on the door of the next room. No answer. I knocked again. Still no answer. By now rather worried, I hammered on the door. As I entered I was greeted with, 'For God's *sake*, man, come on in! I thought you were comin' up from the country you've been so long.' After putting me at my ease in this way, he resumed, 'Well now, I want you to answer a few simple questions about this famous dialogue.' I should say at this point that the book in question was Plato's *Symposium*, a work which explores various aspects of love. I had studied the subject-matter and arguments quite carefully, but this turned out to be a waste of effort. 'First of all, what's the Greek for a cobbler's last?' I shook my head and apologized. Other questions of the same kind followed. 'Now now, this won't do at all, man. Will ye pull yourself together! Here's the easiest of questions. Plato at one point uses a phrase meaning "welcome". What is it?' I remembered dimly that R.G. Bury's commentary had momentarily abandoned its habit of quoting German to say that the Greek for 'welcome' resembled the French *soyez le bienvenu*. So, to break the silence, I reported this irrelevant information. 'Well well,' growled Sir Robert, who was fundamentally a kindly man and wanted his students to do well, 'I'll give you half marks for that.'

Later I learnt that this grotesque procedure was not his own invention but was, rather, a late survival of an old tradition. According to Parke, who had it from Josiah Gilbert Smyly (elected Fellow in 1897), candidates for Fellowship sat in a row for a sort of communal *viva-voce*. On one occasion they were asked, 'What, according to Mr Grote, were the results of the Peloponnesian War?' Each candidate essayed an answer ('The eclipse of Athenian democracy?' 'The rise of Spartan power?' 'The entry of Persia into Greek affairs?'). At every attempt the examiner shook his head. 'No, gentlemen,' he said. 'According to Mr Grote (and now he tapped the desk for emphasis), the results of the Peloponnesian War were *prodigious*!' It's an outrageous story; yet I half believe it. (Certainly Grote *does* refer to the results as prodigious.) And even if it is just an exaggeration, it illustrates a general point. For in the period, say, from 1885–1910 Classics was still the dominant arts subject in the British educational system; and in those years Dublin – with Mahaffy, Tyrrell, Purser, J.B. Bury, and Arthur

Palmer – was one of the foremost centres in the United Kingdom. Yet, along with its more worthy features, the University could still find room for such arid frivolity. It is sometimes said that, when you consider how Classics has been taught in the schools over the centuries, the subject must be intrinsically worthwhile; otherwise it could never have survived. The universities, too, have not been wholly guiltless.

In due course I moved into the ground floor of no. 34 in the New Square, where I shared a large sitting-room and a tiny kitchen with Philip Egerton (an English quaker who had abandoned pacifism and fought against Japan) and Gerry Murphy (who had come to take a degree in Divinity before returning to the army as a chaplain). In the very cold winter of 1947 students had been trapped in a vicious circle. Fires were needed; but since turf was sold by weight, the merchants made sure that every sod was thoroughly soaked. So to dry out the turf one had to have a fire; but to make a fire one had to have turf. To escape from this impasse, students used to pile sods of turf in little mounds on their windowsills – a pathetic expedient. In the late summer of 1948, therefore, I ordered a load of logs. A week later I found a note from Rodway, who was living in no. 34 in the absence of the other two, saying, 'When you look in the coal-hole you will find that you have acquired a *ktema es aei*.' (This was Thucydides' way of describing his great historical work, and it means 'a possession for ever'.) He was right, for the coal-hole was filled to the roof with huge sections of tree-trunks, soaking wet, and thickly encrusted with moss.

For breakfast one ate bread and cereal, bought from the Co-op in Front Square. Milk was delivered daily by Larry with his horse and cart. (The wheels were fitted with pneumatic tyres to help it over the cobblestones.) Benign and rubicund, Larry would remind each student on a Friday of what he owed. When he was told, 'Sorry, Larry, it'll have to wait till next week', he always said, 'Ah sure that's all right.' In the two years that I lived there I never saw anyone actually pay him. For Hughes Brothers Dairy, Trinity College must have been a pretty dud account. In the evening, at commons, we would stand, gowned, behind our chairs while members of staff proceeded to the high table. Then the door would bang shut, and the 'waiter' would hurry up into a pulpit and recite a long Latin grace. (The 'waiter' was a Scholar who was paid £10 a year to perform this duty. Actual waiters were called 'porters'.) After a plate of soup, the main course consisted of large helpings of high-quality meat with two vegetables. Pudding was a more uncertain quantity. One regular item was a long roll of brown suet pudding with raisins in it. This was divided up at the table. Inevitably it was called 'elephant', but the more polite referred to it as 'elephant's trunk'. Rumour had it that Guinness's had offered free stout on condition that the firm might use the College in its advertising; the College in a fit of lunacy had re-fused. So we had to make do with a rather insipid beer. Order usu-ally prevailed; but on one occasion the waiter realized that the only member of staff dining on high table was the Senior Lecturer, the Rev. R.M. Gwynn. Though well liked, Gwynn was now very old and very deaf, a tall white-haired shambling figure, carrying a large ear-trumpet. The student, therefore, decided to take a gamble. He ascended the pulpit, folded his hands, and assumed an expression of piety. Then, for fifteen seconds, he repeated over and over, 'Old Daddy Gwynn thinks I'm saying grace.' He had resumed his seat and was just starting on his soup when a porter appeared at his elbow. 'The Senior Lecturer presents his compliments, sir. He wishes you to know that Old Daddy Gwynn did *not* think you were saying grace. You are fined ten pounds.' (One assumes that, seeing the delighted grins, the old fellow had reached for his ear-trumpet and caught the last few seconds.)

Catering was superintended by Miss Jean Montgomery, a tough old Scot who, though she looked after us very well, was nobody's fool. At the Saturday night hops she used to take the money at the door. One night a student slipped behind the curtains and opened a tall casement window to allow a friend to climb in. All went well until the gate-crasher made the mistake of winning an elimination dance. Then, as he stood with his partner acknowledging the app-lause, Jean Montgomery walked out into the middle of the floor, said, 'Ye didna' pay', and flung him out. When she eventually retired, she was given an honorary MA, much to everyone's de-light. Sadly, she does not appear in the index of the recent history of the College.[22] The lady Professors, however, *are* acknowledged. Constantia Maxwell (History) and Frances Moran (Law) were both to be seen in the late 40s. As pioneers, they had a symbolic significance over and above their importance as individuals.

Dublin University is not often thought of as a progressive institution; yet it conferred degrees on women several years before Oxford and Cambridge. By now, nearly 30 per cent of the undergraduate population were women, and they could be entertained to tea in one's rooms provided one obtained the permission of the Junior Dean. The editor of *TCD*, the student newspaper, once pointed out that, since 'vice' (by which he meant sexual intercourse) could be indulged in during the afternoon, there was really no point in the six o'clock rule. Logically, of course, he was right. But if the editor meant that in *fact* students commonly went to bed together about 4 p.m., and that therefore facilities might as well be extended to midnight, then he was surely misinformed. One has to think back beyond the 70s and the 60s to a time when the age of majority was 21, and the university authorities were held to be *in loco parentis*. For better or worse, the pill had not been invented, and one had to go to some trouble to obtain contraceptives. Over and above all that was the fact that most students (however far they were willing to go) were deterred from intercourse by their principles, or by fear, which is after all a kind of principle. No doubt there were exceptions, especially amongst the worldly wise ex-servicemen and also amongst those who had flats outside College. Yet (though others may have formed a different impression) I myself heard of very few cases; that points to a rather low level of achievement. Nor could I claim that my acquaintances, much as I liked them, were an untypically chaste sample.

As the Library did not lend, most of one's studying went on in the Reading Room – a smallish octagonal building with a domed roof. Above the entrance stood the one word NIKH in Greek capitals, which means Victory – not, as a coach-driver was heard to explain to his group of visitors, 'No Irish Known Here'. After collecting his books from the circulation desk, the student sat rapt in concentration for several hours at a stretch – in theory. Actually he spent an inordinate amount of time watching a parade of characters moving in and out – exhibitionists and notabilities of various kinds, attractive girls (some sporting 'the new look'), eccentric members of staff, and one or two strange old men. One of these last was to be seen most evenings consulting the back numbers of newspapers on a special kind of stand. No more than 5 foot 2, he had a bald head, a sprouting white moustache, and steel-rimmed glasses. He wore an overcoat reaching to his ankles, and moved with the shuffling steps of an octogenarian. No one knew who he was, but in Dublin rumour is always eager to fill such gaps, and some people alleged that he was Argus of the *Evening Herald*. One night when Rodway and I were taking a breather in the front porch, the old fellow came out. My curiosity got the better of me, and I said, 'Excuse me, sir, but are you by any chance Argus of the *Evening Herald*?' 'I'll show you whether or not I'm Argus, you bloody insolent young *pup*!' He then seized my lapels and did his best to hurl me down the steps.

Books classified as pornography had a special catalogue mark. They could not be read without the Librarian's permission, and even then, they were brought only as far as the Long Room, where they would not contaminate other students. As I was preparing a paper on Aldous Huxley for one of the societies, it seemed desirable to read something by D.H. Lawrence, whose anti-intellectualism Huxley found both attractive and repellent. So what better excuse could there be to read *Lady Chatterley*? I duly obtained permission, and waited in the Long Room as an attendant brought the book. I opened it eagerly, and then – dammit! It was the *bowdlerized* edition. Other bibliographical difficulties were of a more structural kind. On a later occasion I wanted to consult a couple of articles in a journal, but as I didn't know exactly what number they were in, I asked an attendant if I might visit the stacks. Very decently, he agreed. As we entered the large eighteenth-century building it looked rather like a glorified hayloft. We went up a staircase and along a corridor, then up a narrower and more rickety set of steps and across a kind of catwalk. By now we were in almost total darkness, and the ranges were so close together that only one person could squeeze in at a time. We stopped, and my guide pointed to a black space. 'It's down there,' he said. 'Third shelf from the bottom. Here's a bicycle lamp.'

Behind the Reading Room were the Fellows' Gardens, which contained a couple of good grass-courts. One afternoon Professor Stanford, with whom our relations as students gradually thawed, asked me to make up a four. I was ready at the gate at 4 p.m., when Stanford arrived with three other people. 'Oh horrors, have I got the sums wrong? Never mind. Perhaps someone wouldn't mind dropping out for the first set.' I volunteered. 'Very good, Rudd. Why not just take a stroll round the Gardens. That's the Library, of course, from an unusual angle; St Patrick's Well is over there by the wall; that pretty little Greek temple is a magnetic observatory …' After wandering around quite happily in the sunshine, thinking what a privilege it was to enjoy such surroundings, I went across to an old sundial in the middle of the lawn. There my eye was caught by some writing, etched indelibly on the brass plate. On close inspection it conveyed a piece of criticism: 'This f—ing thing is three minutes fast'; which supported the rumour that some strange appointments had recently been made to Fellowship.

In my second year the Greek temple was used as the set for a production of Euripides' *Alcestis* in the original. I was cast as a lowly attendant, whose only function (apart from deploring the insensitive carousing of Heracles) was to carry off, along with a colleague, the corpse of Alcestis on a St John's Ambulance stretcher. This posed no problem at first. But on the second day the heavens opened, and the performance was transferred to the Graduates' Memorial Building, where there were three very high steps. To get the bier off stage we had to execute a sort of three-point turn accompanied by a concerted heave. At one frightening moment my fellow-attendant stumbled slightly, canting our load over at a dangerous angle. I saw the dead Alcestis' knuckles go white as she gripped the sides of the stretcher. Just in time, we regained our equilibrium, and the dignity of the Queen (played by the Headmistress of a very OK girls' school) was saved. But one was left with the thought of how easily tragedy could turn into farce – a type of transformation not envisaged by Aristotle.

Alcestis was produced by Barry Roach, who was the leading light in the Dublin University Players. The quality of his work went far towards persuading the Board that the room at the top of no. 6 was no longer adequate, and that the University needed a proper theatre. Other actors and actresses won reputations within the College and also in inter-varsity competitions. But their fame did have limits. One fan was expecting too much when, on being asked for his bus fare, he said, 'Two to Helen Hackman's flat'. It is also perhaps worth adding, in view of the reputation of the Irish as a nation of play-actors, that the most prominent members of Players in those years were either English or else had been to English schools. Students living in the centre of Dublin did not always realize how lucky they were. The main theatres were less than half a mile away. At the Abbey F.J. McCormick and Eileen Crowe performed the Irish classics. The Gate, presided over by the huge and benevolent Lord Longford, housed a range of first-class productions by Hilton Edwards and Michael MacLiammoir, including Shakespeare and Marlowe, Congreve and Sheridan, Tchekov, Ibsen, Wilde and Shaw. When Christopher Fry's verse drama made its brief appearance, it was the Gate that staged *The Lady's Not for Burning*. At the same time the Gaiety played host to visiting companies like the Hamburg State Opera and D'Oyly Carte, as well as staging a wide range of plays. And the Olympia provided everything from grand opera to vaudeville.

One evening, in the white tiled surroundings of Jammet's back bar in Grafton Street, a trio of ex-servicemen began to tell those present about a brilliant magician whom they had just seen at the Olympia. One of his tricks, 'The re-constituted *Herald*', had been particularly impressive. 'This was the way he did it,' said Mike McConville. 'First of all, sir, may I borrow your *Herald*? Would you put a mark on the front page, just to show it's yours. Right. Next he folded it over once, took out a cigarette-lighter, like this; and then set the whole damned thing on fire.' Barman and customers watched in consternation as the *Herald* went up in flames. 'Then, to make absolutely sure there was no deception, he stamped on the ashes, *comme ça*, turning them into powder. And now comes the really clever bit with the magic box ...' 'But Mike,' said a friend, 'you haven't *got* a magic box.' 'God, you're right! Why didn't you say so before?' Then, turning to the company, 'I'm terribly sorry. Something seems to have gone wrong. But believe me, it was a damned good trick!' Things looked as if they might turn ugly but the former owner of the *Herald* agreed to accept 'a ball o' malt' in lieu, and all ended happily.

In those years my friends and I came to know a number of GIs, all totally different from one another, which showed how silly it was to generalize about Americans. Two floors above us, in no. 34, Fred Teahan wrote a PhD thesis on eighteenth-century music. One day he went along to hear a lecture on the subject by his supervisor, and found that most of the material came from the section which he had submitted the previous week. His emotions were much the same as those of Lucky Jim, when he found that his work on shipbuilding had been used by L.S. Caton to obtain a Chair at the University of Tucuman. One of our classmates, James O'Keefe, soon began to skip Sir Robert Tate's composition seminars ('You don't get no laughs from Bobby'). Then he disappeared from other classes too. A week after that, he gave back the key of his rooms and collected the deposit, carefully leaving the door open. He then returned with a small van, loaded on as much College furniture as he could, and sold it on the quays. I doubt if it paid his fare to the boat.

I cannot claim to have known J.P. Donleavy (for some reason 'Mike' to his friends); but I remember him as a rather reticent man in a brown corduroy jacket. In those days he was a painter rather than a writer. I do not recall any reports of a Rabelaisian lifestyle, but he must already have had some sort of reputation. One day in the very old lavatories near Pearse Street gate I noticed an extremely primitive version of the human genitalia pencilled onto the white-washed wall. A week later someone had put a frame round the drawing and added 'Donleavy pinxit'. A week later again, a third hand had supplied a sociological comment: 'The ginthry, begob!' I add as a sequel that ten years later, when lecturing in North America, I noticed a very large man with closely clipped red hair and a stubbly beard. He watched me intently but didn't appear to take any notes. At the end he came up and seized my hand. 'Hey, I just wanted to shake the hand of a man from Trinity College Dublin!' 'Really? Have you some interest in the place?' 'I sure have.' 'Are you working on Swift ... or Goldsmith?' 'Nope.' 'Burke, perhaps, or Berkeley?' 'No. None of those guys.' 'So what's the attraction, then?' '*The Ginger Man!*' he roared. 'I wanna get to meet J.P. Donleavy. What a *genius!*'

Other students, too, were destined to make their names as writers, like William Trevor, Jennifer Johnston, and Harry Keating. Also, though he was not an undergraduate, and would have thought it an act of treachery to become one, Brendan Behan spoke at meetings from time to time, and occasionally showed up at parties. *Borstal Boy* and *The Quare Fellow* were still in the future, but some people already found him impressive. Others recoiled from his deliberately swinish behaviour. Friends of his, like John Ryan, have written regretfully about this aspect of his personality; but clearly, as with Dylan Thomas, it had deep psychological roots and could not be willed away. Students, of course, don't know or care much about other people's potential – quite rightly. You are valued, or otherwise, for what you are at the time. In any given period the professional schools will turn out a certain number of future judges, bishops and consultants. But they are not necessarily the people who were most interesting as undergraduates. Arts students are even less predictable. Sometimes one can make guesses. It seemed quite likely, for instance, that Deirdre MacSharry, with her charm and vivacity, would become an actress or a 'media personality'. In fact she was to make a successful career in the world of women's magazines. Dermot Englefield, an historian, talked enthusiastically about art, and his friends learnt a good deal from him in late-night coffee-sessions. None of us imagined he would become Librarian of the House of Commons; and even if we had, it would have seemed quite irrelevant. In a few cases, however, a student could be seen to have started on a career before leaving College. One man returned from the war as a Major with an MC; he was an inter-varsity boxing champion and captain of rugger; and it was clear that he had what are now called 'managerial skills'. On graduating, he went along to consult A.J. Levanthal, who, in addition to lecturing in French, worked part time in the careers office. 'What qualifications do you have?' 'A general Arts degree and an LLB.' 'Ah well, hmm. In that case you may find it quite hard to get anything satisfactory in the way of a job.' Thirty-five years later, Sir David Orr retired as Chairman of Unilever Ltd. (Not long after the consultation, Levanthal, who was uneasy as an academic and more at home in the world of literary magazines, left Dublin and became Beckett's secretary in Paris, just as, years before, Beckett had left the same lecturing post in Trinity to work for Joyce.)

Finally, there was a very small category of people who didn't seem to be going anywhere, but who, without any effort on their part, were accepted as 'characters'. One of these was Eoin (Owen) O'Mahony, known universally as The Pope. By now in his mid forties, the Pope had been Auditor of the Historical Society in 1930 and was said to have had a brilliant but eccentric career at the bar. It was now unclear what he did; but no one bothered to enquire, for the man bubbled over with information – not about himself, but about Irish life, especially Irish families and Irish politics.[23] As a genealogist, the Pope had a huge card-index, or data retrieval system, inside his head. One felt sure he could have dictated a work like MacLysaght's *Irish Families* quite spontaneously over a few pints. Naturally enough, much of his conversation was quite scandalous. 'Ah yes. Poor Seamus was the third son of the Connaught branch of the family. Once he gave up his career as a mercenary he began to go to the bad. His wife Molly (one of the O'Brindleys of Ballintober) used to say, I'm always relieved when Seamus comes home footless, because then I know he's been faithful.' His lore about politics always seemed to come from inside. Thus a casual conversation in Front Square might have ended like this, '... Of course when Seán MacBride resigned from the IRA in 1939 it was for reasons never officially disclosed. It all began with a remark of Stephen Hayes's – oh, but I'll tell you about that later. Look, there's Bedell Stanford. I must go and get him to intervene on behalf of that poor Basque nationalist who was sentenced last week.' And off he would go. (Stanford, it should be explained, was a member of the Irish Senate.)

O'Mahony's income, which was said to come from property in Co. Cork, was highly uncertain. Sometimes he had nowhere to go and would ask to be put up for a couple of nights in one's rooms. There were days when he even seemed to be without the price of a meal, and would happily tuck into one's cheese and scrambled eggs. But then, unpredictably, his ship would come in. Once in London, after a match against London Irish, the team came off the field to find the short bearded figure of the Pope standing at the entrance to the pavilion. He greeted me and a team-mate, and then said, 'Would you care to have dinner at my club tomorrow evening? Good. Let's say 7.30, then, in the vestibule of the National Liberal.' The Pope duly showed up and addressed the doorman, who clearly recognized him, 'Good evening, Ambrose.'

At the same time he handed Ambrose a raincoat which looked as if it had been borrowed from one of the less affluent characters in a Beckett play. When he led the way to the bar, it became plain that either a large pen, or else a small bottle of ink, had leaked in the hip pocket of his grey trousers, so that, as he walked in front, one ultramarine buttock kept peeping from under his jacket. If other members noticed, they were far too discreet to pass comment, and we had a very jolly evening.

Societies offered such a wealth of choice that one had to try to discriminate; and sometimes, inevitably, one got it wrong. Once I went to hear Mr F. La T. Godfrey, a Hegelian, give a paper to the Metaphysical Society. His first sentence was, 'I propose to treat of moral obligation as an element in rational experience.' To my shame, that was the only sentence I understood. On another occasion a student persuaded Lennox Robinson to come over from the Abbey to speak to a paper on Yeats. To stimulate the visitor, the student said a few rather harsh things about his subject, 'superstitious ... anti-rational ... fascist ... snob, etc.' These tactics proved disastrous. Instead of being goaded into an eloquent fury, poor Lennox simply stood there, tall and terribly thin, wringing his hands and repeating again and again, 'How *could* you? How *could* you?' Most of the meetings, however, were lively affairs. On special occasions, guests would be invited over from England, and one heard speeches from people as diverse as Middleton Murry, Elizabeth Bowen, Harold Nicolson, and Herbert Butterfield. It was a matter of some pride, however, that local personalities like Owen Sheehy Skeffington, David Webb, and R.B. McDowell were always the equal of the visitors in eloquence and wit. Sometimes, too, students would come to speak at inter-varsity debates. These functions would be followed by the usual celebrations. There is always a chance, I suppose, that, if you lend your bedroom to a guest, you will find next morning that he has thrown up on your carpet. Statistically, perhaps, it is not a very *large* chance. All I will say here is that I was unlucky. It was some compensation, then, to represent one of the TCD societies at a debate in St Andrews. The old Aer Lingus Dakota ran into a storm which threw it around the sky, but I accepted that as normal, for it was my first time in an aeroplane. At St Andrews the students' bright red gowns stood out against the grey stone; a bitter wind whipped in from the sea; and ruined churches proclaimed the ravages of time and John Knox. I remember, with an inner groan, that at the debate, which had to do with nationalism, I presented the speaker with a symbolic revolver to show that Mr Costello, in his words, had 'taken the gun out of Irish politics'. Oh dear.

Because of its central position, College Park was a favourite venue for big athletic meetings. These were still the days of grass tracks, straddle jumps and bamboo poles; and if there was any seating it was never more than a temporary affair of planks and scaffolding. Still, the Dublin crowds saw performances by some world-famous athletes, like MacDonald Bailey, Arthur Wint, and Sidney Wooderson. And every now and then an Irishman would emerge with exceptional ability; one thinks of Bert Healion (hammer), John Joe Barry (mile), and Jimmy Reardon (440 yards). There was an apocryphal story that one evening, when a policeman's headgear was stolen, the thief ran off at such an astonishing speed that the Gardai knew it was Jimmy Reardon. The College Races, which took place in the Park every summer term, were traditionally both a serious athletics meeting, at which the College Championships were run off, and a fashionable social occasion (people in morning suits and smart dresses enjoying strawberries and hock in a marquee). One year a couple of ex-servicemen had the idea of introducing a marathon, which would start in Co. Wicklow and be reported over the loudspeaker as it drew closer to Dublin; it would then end with a circuit of the track in the College Park. The event was duly advertised in the programme, and in the course of the afternoon bulletins were issued, saying how far the runners had got and who was leading. In fact the competitors had enjoyed a boozy lunch in the Lincoln's Inn at the back gate, and were now happily relaxing in the pavilion. Shortly after 4 p.m. they donned various kinds of outlandish gear, and, when announced, straggled onto the track. I remember someone wheeling me round in a barrow. To judge from the derisive jeers, the trick was successful enough, but there was no denying that from a purist's standpoint it lowered the tone of the occasion.

Tennis was a minority interest. The College's courts were second-rate; and, appropriately, we competed in the second level of the Dublin League. Within our small numbers were people from England, Sweden and Kenya; and my doubles partner one year in the College championships (the only time I ever won anything) came from Port Said. Except in 1950, we lost to University College Dublin in the annual McCabe Cup competition. They had Joe Hackett, who in the post-war years succeeded Cyril Kemp as Ireland's number one. But Joe would not have beaten England's Tony Mottram, who played at Fitzwilliam on a couple of occasions. And he in his turn ranked significantly below the Australians Dinny Pails and Geoff Brown, who also took part in the Fitzwilliam tournament. In those years Dublin was visited by the Americans Louise Brough and Doris Hart, and a little later by Maureen Connolly ('Little Mo'). So the Irish had an opportunity to see just how low they ranked in the tennis hierarchy.

In rugby things were otherwise, as was shown when Ireland won the Triple Crown in 1948 and 49. Those teams reflected the strength of Queen's University, which had taken over from Old Belvedere as the most stylish and successful club in the country. But Old Belvedere still supplied Des O'Brien at no. 8, and the captain Karl Mullen. The latter did not have the squat massive build of the typical hooker. He was so flexible about the hips that in the scrum he could point forward with his trunk while gathering his feet up underneath him and twisting so as to face the incoming ball. While this must have imposed a strain on his prop forwards it gave him a very high success rate. His legs, one may add, were protected by special, surgically made shinguards. Because he was slightly taller than most front-row forwards, Mullen was also effective at the front of the line-out. Having made a catch, he would turn his back to the opposition and protect the ball by holding it down between his shins. From there he would hand it back to the scrum-half. The Irish scrum-half was the gifted, but ill-starred Ernie Strathdee, whose long passes helped Jack Kyle to show his brilliance. Strathdee at this time was a Presbyterian minister in Ulster. It also happened that in the Irish-English match of 1949, one of the Irish centres was a Catholic priest called T.J. Gavin. On the morning of the match a newspaper article commented on the unusual phenomenon of a rugby priest. A photo appeared with the article, producing an interesting ecclesiastical composite named

The Dublin University Philosophical Society Committee of 1950.
Back row, l. to r.: Steele, Wicken, Bailey, Hine, Cleary, Erimona, Rudd.
Front row: Cookman, Burleigh, Mills, Sweeting, Kenny.

Dublin University XV *vs* Steele-Bodger's XV, 1950.
Back row, l. to r.: Mr Thompson (referee), Griffin*, Crowe*, Lane, O'Neill*,
Lynn, Dargan, Rudd, Mullan*, Gaston*, Lane. *Middle*: Rogers, Browne,
Hamilton, McVicker, Bell*, Moran, Fitzgerald, Knott, Sweetman, Pollock,
Crane. *Front*: Browne*, Roe*, Warren, Devine, Mullen, Warke, Steele-Bodger
(Capt.)*, Moyan, Hayes, Kingsmill-Moore. [* *denotes international*]

Father Strathdee. To complete the ecumenical effect, the actual photo was of the Church of Ireland parson, Austin Carry, a player who, had it not been for the war, would surely have been capped for Ireland.

Like several hundred others, I played with or against those men at club level only; there was never any doubt that I belonged to the infrastructure of the game. To a scrum-half who had scuttled around behind a pack of large eighteen-year olds, and who was still well under ten stone, senior rugby was literally 'a whole new ball-game'. When I was setting off on a Saturday, my good mother used to say, 'Remember now, if a nasty big man comes to tackle you, throw the ball away!' I always did my best to obey her. The Dublin grounds provided a wide range of ordeals – toiling up the hill against the wind in Clontarf, flopping about after torrential rain in the evil quagmire of College Park, sweltering in a spring cup-tie at Lansdowne Road. Out of town games brought their own hazards. Once a group of us who couldn't afford to stay overnight in Limerick had to catch a milk train, which left at about 10 p.m. and then, after clanking slowly across Ireland and stopping at every halt to take on more churns, arrived at Kingsbridge about 3.30 a.m. Before I left the dinner which followed the match, a Limerick man had said to me, 'Are you on the square?' I took this odd expression to mean the same as 'Are you on the level?' and I couldn't think what he meant. When he saw my bafflement he said, 'Oh never mind. It was just a thought.' I later found out that this was an enquiry whether I was a freemason. If I'd only been quick enough I might have got myself a comfortable bed. Instead, there I was in a very old and very Spartan railway carriage with about half-a-dozen team-mates. A few minutes before we were due to leave, our hooker (a Belfast man) waltzed through the barrier with an armful of stout-bottles. Making his way to the driver's cab, he said, 'There's a wee bottle for yew, my friend; and there'll be another if you get us to Dublin on time.' Then he came back down the platform to the ticket collector. 'Have one on me! And if any pretty girls arrive show them to this carriage here.' Just as the whistle was about to blow, a vast woman, heavily laden, presented her ticket. The porter immediately took her by the elbow and propelled her across to our carriage. 'There you are now. You'll find

some young men in there to look after you' – this with a conspira-
torial leer. Luckily someone had the presence of mind to seize her
cases and carry them into the corridor. 'I'm afraid this is a rowdy
lot, ma'am; let me find you a quieter seat.' With that, the bemused
woman was bundled into the next compartment, much to her relief I am sure.

On the team's English tour in 1949 we went first to Cambridge. After the game we were taken to the University Arms for a
meal. A couple of hours later, someone noticed that the walls were
decorated with items of antique armour. One of our wings, Derry
Unwin, put on a helmet which completely covered his head. Before he could get it off again, someone shouted through the visor,
'Hey, is it any good? Can you feel this?' At the same time he
brought down a fifteenth-century halberd on the crown of the
helmet. Someone else followed with a lance. 'Try this!', and a
third with the flat of a sabre, 'Have at you, then!' By now the hel-
meted Unwin was reeling around the dining room, and might well
have suffered worse damage had not the management stepped in:
'Now gentlemen please, your fun is going too far.' Which reminded me that, when the puritans put an end to bear-baiting, it was to
stop the tormentors' pleasure rather than the bear's pain. After
playing Headingly in Leeds we came south again to meet London
Irish. Our opponent's pack that day included my dear old friend
Tommy Headon. It was ten years since he had played against
Wales at Ravenhill; and now, with his stockings down and his
jersey outside his pants, he was expanding into an early but majestic middle age. For the first fifteen minutes of each half he dominated the forward play; after that, he rested gently in the set
scrums, and instead of following the ball around the pitch, he
made for where he thought it was going. And very often he was
right. After the game he made an amusing speech, which included
a reference to myself. 'Twenty years ago I used to dandle him on
my knee, and now the little bugger is running in and out between
my legs.' Universally liked and admired, Tommy was one of the
game's great personalities, and I was proud to be teased by him.
Alas, I never saw him again.

In one of the years when Oxford came to Dublin, it was pointed
out that if a party of sixteen or more males showed up at the dance

in the Metropole there would be a rather acute shortage of wo-men. So, as I happened to be organizing the dance, I rang around, following up various contacts, and, by what might be called a piece of innocent pimping, provided about ten dancing-partners for the visitors. That, as it happened, worked out very well. But after the dance one had to reckon with the Knights' breakfast. This was a function laid on in College by the Knights of the Campanile, a social club formed specially to entertain visiting teams. Some poor dupe invariably agreed to lend his rooms for the purpose, and now, about 3.30 a.m., twenty or more slightly battered revellers arrived looking for bacon and eggs. The food was duly provided. The problems began when people started to do their party tricks. For example, an Oxford second row forward was blessed with a flat spot on the top of his head. This enabled him to place a full pint of beer there, to march around the table while his team-mates chant-ed, 'Do you know the muffin man?', climb onto the table, and finally descend again without spilling a drop. Unfortunately, this was seen as a challenge by one of the home team who did not have the necessary type of skull.

As September 1950 approached, thoughts turned reluctantly to finals. It was an uninviting prospect, for Part II of Moderatorship was arranged in a way which took no account of the students' mental state. There was a three-hour paper on Monday morning, and another in the afternoon. The same pattern was repeated on Tuesday and Wednesday and Thursday and Friday. Then, as a concluding flourish, there were orals on the Saturday morning. Not surprisingly, one of the best students in our year broke down on the Saturday and had to be taken to hospital. There were other defects too. One has been described already – the excessive stress on memory-work. In one of the orals the Professor of Latin (a most affable man) said, 'Tell me about the manuscripts of Quintil-ian.' Again, several of the papers very properly included essay-questions. Yet at no time in our four-year course had we received any tuition in writing essays. It was just assumed that we could do it when required. However, granted that the system of examina-tion was faulty, there were various ways of dealing with it. One chap in another course dashed into the exam, seized the paper, and began to write furiously. Ten minutes later came the sound of a script being crumpled into a ball, followed by 'Oh God! That character's not in *Phèdre!*' A new sheet was taken, and again sparks flew from the student's pen. Then, after another ten minutes, 'Oh God, she *is!*' Very different was the technique of my friend Alec Dalzell, who during a paper on classical architecture was to be seen gazing out of the window. He later explained that he had been studying the entablature of the Bank of Ireland.

As an *alma mater* passes judgment on her students, so they, in their impertinence, judge her. Apart from the points made already, Trinity's shortcomings were mostly due to poverty. This could be seen in the state of her buildings and furniture, in the lack of sports facilities, in the limited purchase of American and continental books, in the shortage (as I was told) of scientific equipment, and in the uncompetitive rates of staff pay. Beyond that, while parochialism in appointments was no longer evident, there was a kind of *academic* parochialism – we rarely shared meetings with University College or Maynooth; and (at least in my subject) there was never an Irish dimension. Finally, one suspects there was a certain blindness on the part of the authorities to student misery, whether financial, emotional or academic. I cannot recall anyone receiving counselling or psychological help, and I don't think there was a University health service as such. If wrong about this, it indicates a similar blindness in myself.

These few defects (as it seemed to me) were heavily outweighed by Trinity's attractions. College life went on within a safe and civilized urban environment; I never heard of a student being mugged or raped. Government interference was minimal. And although financially the College always seemed about to go down the drain, especially in 1948–51 when the unsympathetic Mr McGilligan was Minister of Finance, it never actually did. Internally, though a few scholars were wastefully employed in administration, at least no one could complain of an officious and top-heavy bureaucracy. From 1946–50 the student population, though still no more than 2000, was larger and more diverse than ever before. According to McDowell and Webb, by 1952 30 per cent of students came from Great Britain, 18 per cent from Northern Ireland, 18 per cent from overseas, and only 34 per cent from the Republic. As fees did not cover costs, this put an unfair burden on the taxpayer. Nevertheless, the social and intellectual gain was immense. More recently, Trinity has had to cope with the opposite problem – that of excessive provincialism. Again, the College was sometimes accused of complacency. That charge is always hard to as-sess, for others will label the same attitude as 'healthy local pride'. My own impression is that there was far less complacency in Trinity than in several universities that I have seen since. (Another critic will retort that this may have been because we had little to be complacent about.) But at any rate there was none of the institutionalized bragging and self-advertisement which have become so familiar in Britain and America in the last decade. For the stud-ents, good food and drink were cheap, and entertainment was readily available. There was enough leisure and freedom to allow people to try their hand variously. You didn't have to be particularly *good* at anything; it was all part of education; and if you happened to be secretary or treasurer of a club, you might even pick up some practical experience. If the Board had been asked its opinion (not that it ever *was*), it would probably have said that the most important components of education for an arts student were lib-rary, friends, and staff – in that order. In memory, however, the order is different. Friends come first. And while every ageing graduate has his or her set of mental videos, all have this in common: the actors have not yet donned the ridiculous disguise that people assume in middle age (the grey hair, the padded stomachs, the wrinkled faces); they appear as students really are – perennially young.

Notes and Bibliography

1   Under the heading 'Mon. 18th, 8 a.m., Dublin Bay', the crew's record says: 'Here Irwin took over for the Forenoon Watch and flew the ship in majestic sweeps over his native land and city' (Masefield, 142). Flight Lieut. H. Carmichael Irwin was killed, with 47 others, when the R101 crashed in France on 5 October 1930. This is one of the few pieces of verification I have done. In the main this is not a work of research but a collection of reminiscences. So I apologize in advance for inaccurate dates, misspelt names, and other mistakes of detail. As for the silliness, that, I hope, will be seen as an attempt to recall the perspective of my first childhood rather than as a sign of my second.

I should like to thank my friend Joan Polden (not the cousin of that name who is mentioned in the book) for producing a typescript of high professional quality.

2   Blake, p.233 n.1.

3   For figures, see Blake, p.68 n.1.

4   Blake, p.235, n.1.

5   See Fisk, pp.451–2.

6   *Ibid.*, p.250 and notes 55 and 56.

7   See, for example, Cave Brown, index under Enigma and Ultra, and the relevant items in his bibliography.

8   See Fisk, Chap.12, especially pp.390–2 and pp.400–2. The unemployment figures are given by Blake, Appendix 1.

9   Share, p.53.

10 Fisk, Chap.7.

11 *Ibid.*, pp.252–5, 269–72.

12 *Ibid.*, pp.435–6.

13 *Ibid.*, pp.421–2.

14 *Ibid.*, pp.129–33.

15 *Ibid.*, pp.151–2, 282–6.

16 See also Fisk, pp.291, 302.

17 Share, p.139.

18 Patrick Campbell, as quoted in Inglis, p.47.

19 Quoted with the kind permission of *The Irish Times*. A full-length study of the editor is now available. See *Mr Smyllie, Sir* by Tony Gray.

20 McDowell and Webb, pp.470–1, 504.
21 A clear account of events leading to the election of Dr A.A. McConnell as Provost in 1952 is given in McDowell and Webb.
22 Nor does she figure in the index of the new history of the College by J.V. Luce.
23 For a slightly surrealistic version of one of the Pope's disquisitions, see Ryan, pp.85–8.

Blake, John W., *Northern Ireland in the Second World War* (Belfast 1956)

Cave Brown, Anthony, *Bodyguard of Lies* (London 1976)

Fisk, Robert, *In Time of War* (London 1983)

Gray, Tony, *Mr Smyllie, Sir* (Dublin 1991)

Inglis, Brian, *West Briton* (London 1962)

Luce, J.V., *Trinity College Dublin – The First 400 Years* (Dublin 1992)

McDowell, R.B. and Webb, D.A., *Trinity College Dublin, 1592–1952* (Cambridge 1982)

Masefield, Peter, *To Ride the Storm* (London 1982)

Ryan, John, *Remembering How We Stood* (Dublin 1975, Mullingar 1987)

Share, Bernard, *The Emergency: Neutral Ireland 1939–45* (Dublin 1978)

Stephan, Enno, *Spies in Ireland* (London 1965)